MW01611990

101 Paleo Slow Cooker Recipes:

Easy, Delicious, Gluten-free Hands-Off Cooking For Busy People

PUBLISHED BY:

Dan Thompson

Copyright © 2014

Written By: Dan Thompson

Just to say "Thank You!" for purchasing this book,

I want to give you a gift

%100 Absolutely Free

My top 10 favourite Paleo recipes

Click here to get your free gift!

Or go to http://paleolifestyleguide.com/

Table of Contents

Introduction

Food is the fuel that keeps us running, but we don't want to spend our lives thinking about healthy food choices and cooking. There is a lot more to do than just cook and it's easy to walk in the shop, grab something ready-made and eat it. Unfortunately unhealthy food choices result in health issues such as obesity and lacking in energy, and when we have to switch to strict diets to save our own health, it gives us headache – it's hard.

There really is something special about the Paleo diet and slow cooking; this combination doesn't tie you to kitchen allowing you to enjoy the best and rest of your life. The Paleo diet is healthy, it ensures that you to get all the necessary vitamins your body needs without making you obese and is isn't restricting in terms of allowing you to enjoy delicious foods. Does a grain-free, dairy-free way of eating sound challenging and not particularly satisfying? Dive into this book to discover the world of Paleo slow cooking!

In this book you will find out about what the Paleo diet really is, what you can and can't eat, what healthy alternatives there are to replace the unhealthy foods you've already used to eating, and the most important thing, recipes to help you get established eating the Paleo slow cooker way. These recipes ask for 1 to 15 minutes of your precious time to prepare ingredients for the slow cooker. The magic of the slow cooker is that it allows you to prepare foods in amounts that feed your family and cater for a variety of taste buds. The useful thing about the slow cooker, is that it does the work even while you are sleeping. The trick with the Paleo diet and why some people can't really stick to it is that information about it is sometimes fairly contradictory: experts say that potatoes and beans are not Paleo, while many slow cooker recipes labeled under "Paleo" contain these foods. This issue is solved in this book as we let you in on 101 fully Paleo recipes your slow cooker that will turn into delicious foods.

No wonder the Paleo diet and slow cookers have boomed in their popularity - it's a match made in heaven, so let's get started on this Paleo journey!

What is the Paleo Diet?

The Paleo diet has other popular names such as "the cave-man diet", and "the Paleolithic or Stone-Age diet". These names clearly explain what it's all about. The Paleo diet is all about eating the way our ancestors did way back. Those brave men and strong women lived without all that comfort we have now and without all these foods that make us fat or do not provide the necessary vitamins for healthy living. We are talking about the foods that hunters-gatherers ate, not farmers who are able to grow food because of the developments in agriculture. While many people turn to vegan diets discovering that they don't get everything that their bodies require, the Paleo diet is a healthy way to keep off excess weight and to address many health issues ensuring that you get what your body needs.

This diet ensures a high intake of vitamins, antioxidants, protein, minerals, fiber, potassium and healthy fats, such as Omega 3 and a low sodium and carbohydrate intake. Basically it means that your diet will include exactly what you need and exclude what is not necessary for your body, mind and wellness in general.

Many people nowadays have health and especially weight issues because they are lactose and gluten intolerant. This diet is free of both lactose and gluten. Your diet will consist of fruits, vegetables, meat, healthy oils, seafood, eggs, roots and seeds and great variety of natural spices, but you will exclude dairy products, refined sugar, grains and cereals, refined vegetable oils, potatoes, legumes like peanuts, beans, peas and lentils, pasta and unhealthy processed foods. It's not as difficult as it might sound at the beginning. Once you start with the Paleo diet, you will definitely feel a lot better and will therefore not think about giving it up. The Paleo diet requires only one thing from you: knowledge of what you're eating. This means that you acknowledge what actually allows your body to function properly and what is tasty, healthy food.

You might have heard that eating red meat can increase the chance of getting cancer or heart disease. Well, modern science has something else to say: get rid of these beliefs. Cooking red meat in improper way really might harm your health, for example, if you cook it in a pan with a lot of salt and refined vegetable oil or butter. So, yes, that's the key: the preparation of your food!

One more enjoyable fact is that the Paleo diet is neither too fat, nor tasteless, nor does it require that you live without the tastes that you love. Eradicating sugar from your meals does not mean that you won't get sweet tastes through the food you eat in the Paleo diet. In the same way, no longer consuming dairy products does not mean that you won't get enough of calcium, because there are many other and a lot healthier products that will provide you with the necessary amount of calcium. We will talk more about products ideal for the Paleo diet in the following chapters.

Oh, and if you like to exercise, the Paleo diet ensures that your workouts are a lot more effective! It means that the same exercise that you do, even the simplest form of exercise, such as those daily actions that include taking stairs, walking or gardening in your backyard, will bring far better results!

What about your eating schedule and how to fit it in with your agenda? It's easy: you eat when you want to eat. Cavemen did not eat after looking at the clock – they ate when they wanted to eat.

Cavemen also didn't count calories. If you feel happier doing so, feel free to count them; you will find the calorie count for each recipe here in this book, but remember that your body actually tells you how much you need if you stick to healthy food. The Paleo diet is nutritious and fulfilling enough to keep you away from storing unwanted fat in your body.

So, let's get going!

What is slow cooking?

The Paleo diet includes a lot of tasty raw foods, but you might already know how to deal with these – wash, cut and eat. This, however, does not mean that you'll only be able to eat cold foods. All the recipes you will find in this book are all for food prepared in slow cooker or a so-called crock-pot. It's not just healthy, but truly tasty as well, and most of the recipes do not require that you stand staring at the food while it's cooking and stirring it every 3 minutes.

Slow cooking means simmering and preparing food on relatively low temperatures – a very gentle method in which to cook food. The catch as to why slow cooking is so much healthier than other cooking methods is that it makes food a lot more tender and the nutrient content of vegetables does not decrease as much as it does when cooking food outwith a slow cooker. The Paleo diet food cooked in a slow cooker does not lose as many vitamins in comparison to fast cooking on a high heat and along with that, the flavors of the ingredients you use mix well in a slow cooker so you get to experience new and enjoyable tastes. What slow cooking really means is less time on preparation and more on cooking to make sure that you gain as much as possible from your food. One more very important thing is that slow cooking is absolutely great for preparing large amounts of food: a slow cooker cooks large pieces of meat thoroughly while you are working out, while you are at work or on your way to collect children from school. Slow cooking ensures that your life doesn't stop to prepare meals.

Why the Paleo diet and slow cooking are a match made in heaven!

One thing that scares many people is that slow cooking means you can't just run into your kitchen, drop whatever you have in the refrigerator into a pan, and eat it within a few minutes. This shouldn't be something that you're worrying about: the Paleo diet doesn't mean that whatever you have from now on you will only prepare in your slow cooker. This book offers instructions for the healthiest Paleo diet recipes that are as easy and convenient as putting all the ingredients into one pot and then leaving! Return after few hours and enjoy your meal, or have your food ready to reheat and enjoy later on! In fact, the Paleo diet and slow cooking are a match made in heaven and here's why:

- It's healthy (you already know this);
- It's easy and you do not need to be an amazing chef to achieve delicious results;
- Slow cooking your Paleo diet food is a way to prepare your food for more than just one day or one person;
- You can do whatever you wish as your slow cooker does the work for you because your food doesn't require attention while it's cooking;
- You will discover more natural tastes;
- You can prepare large pieces of meat without overdoing them and/or drying out the meat;
- When you come home from work, a freshly cooked, healthy, warm meal is there waiting for you;
- You can make many different dishes using the same ingredients that can be found easily, for example, carrots;
- The meals are so nutritious that you are naturally kept away from overeating, and, as a consequence, gaining weight and

causing health problems;

- Your energy levels increase and this therefore helps you to lose excess weight;
- Paleo slow cooking provides you with different kinds of healthy foods: warm, cold, tender, spicy, mild, bite-sized, light, hearty, and large amounts of food cooked thoroughly; and
- You'll maintain your shape without too much effort.

How slow cooking saves you time and money

- Electric crock-pots for slow cooking are not too expensive, and they are absolutely safe to leave them plugged into electricity for a long period of time while you are not around.
- A slow-cooker uses electricity and saves you money as it doesn't use more electric power than a light bulb.
- You are not required to spend a lot to vary your meals and there is no need for you to buy expensive ingredients to experience new tastes. Slow cooking does the job of bringing out new flavors for you.
- You will save money that you previously spent on unhealthy, processed foods. Following your old diet, you would have also had to have spent more money on restoring your health in an attempt to repair the damage you may have caused.
- Slow cooking asks for a few minutes of your time to prepare the ingredients and that's it. While the food is cooking, you are free to do whatever you need to do. If time is money, a slow-cooker provides you with that.
- A slow cooker enables you to make delicious food using readily available and cheap ingredients, such as vegetables. Cheap can taste just as great if you give it a try and simmer it in a slow cooker.
- Slow cooking saves your time and money because you cut expenses on solving health issues – this diet keeps you healthy.

What you need – equipment

The main thing here is a slow cooker or a crock-pot - an electronic device with a ceramic bowl and lid. Crock-pots are really easy to use, you can regulate the heat and cooking time, and it's safe to leave them for long time when you're not at home. Using a crock-pot honestly makes life a lot easier.

If you do not have an electric slow-cooker just yet, there are alternatives you can use in which you can steam and simmer foods on a low heat:

-   Dutch oven – a pot with tight walls and a lid. You will obtain the best results by placing it in the oven.
-   Casserole dish – a deep saucepan to cook food, again in the oven.
-   Regular (oven-proof) pot – you can heat this either in oven or on low-heat on your gas or electric stove, but you will have to stir it from time to time so that the food doesn't stick to the walls of the pot or burn the bottom of the pot.

With these alternatives in mind, you can still achieve the same delicious results as if you were using an electric device, but some dishes just might ask for some more attention during the cooking process.

For some dishes, you will need a pan to brown the ingredients to obtain some different flavors and to maintain consistency before putting them into the electric slow cooker (or its alternatives).

Some other recipes call for foil or parchment paper to place in the slow cooker, of for you to use a blender, food processor, or toothpicks.

Other pieces of equipment that you require are every day kitchen items such as a knife, fork, grater, etc.

What you need – products

So, finally we are here, nearing those delicious Paleo recipes.

Here's a quick reminder of products that you definitely won't need and that **are NOT used in a Paleo diet**:

- Sugar: this means any kind of brown, white or other refined sugar and candy. Alternatives to refined sugars that are used in the Paleo diet are maple syrup or honey, but remember, you use these in small doses and they are not for everyday use.
- Legumes: beans, peas, lentils and peanuts.
- Grains: corn, wheat, barley, oatmeal, rye, rice and others. It means that you will have to exclude flour and also products such as muffins, pancakes, pizza, pasta and bread. You will, however, learn how to make bread without using grain flour in this book.
- Starch vegetables: yams and potatoes are a no-no, although many people support using sweet potatoes in a Paleo diet. And, yes, you really don't need potato chips to be healthy in life!
- Dairy products: milk, all kinds of cheese, butter and yoghurt, cream and ice-cream. Stone-age people used milk only to feed infants, and they didn't acquire milk from any species of animal. Milk is really only necessary for infants and even they don't drink milk from other species when a mother breastfeeds, right?
- Salt: salted fish and meat products such as salami, etc are not allowed. You won't feel as though you're missing out on salt though because the Paleo diet offers its own alternative to refined salt, and that is sea salt.

- And add to this list all artificially sweetened fruit and berry juices, ketchup, mayonnaise, soft drinks and soda drinks from the supermarket shelves because they are packed with sugar and preservatives that your body has no need for.

Don't be worrying! The list of what you CAN eat is a lot longer!

This is what a healthy, delicious, and nutritious Paleo diet advises you to **include in your menu**:

- **Meat:** beef, pork, turkey, duck, chicken and other poultry; lamb, goat, and rabbit. When purchasing meat, the best option is always grass-fed meat and if you're one to worry about calories and fat, you should trim off any excess fat. As long as the meat you buy is not processed in an unhealthy way with added artificial preservatives, it has a place on your table. Organ meat such as tongue, kidney, liver, heart and marrow are welcome as well!
- **Seafood, fish and shellfish**: salmon, tuna, herring, eel, trout, mackerel, crab, mussels, lobster, oysters, shrimp, octopus, squid, shark, swordfish, roe and others are all great, just make sure that you buy your seafood products from a safe source and avoid all canned fish meat.
- **Mushrooms:** cremini, Portobello, shiitake, bolete, chanterelle, rehishi, maitake, porchini and other mushrooms are all fine for you to eat.
- **Fruits, vegetables and leafy greens:** apples, apricots, kiwis, lemons, mangos, melons, nectarines, pears, oranges, pineapples, watermelon, grapefruit, avocados, arugula, artichokes, different kinds of peppers, tomatoes, pumpkins, rhubarb, squashes, asparagus, broccoli, Brussels sprouts,

cabbage, endives, grapes, leeks, olives, cauliflower, cucumber, eggplant, onion greens, spinach, zucchini, etc. The list is endless. The main thing is to ensure that you buy these foods unprocessed. Do take into account that buying raisins, dried plums, apricots or other dried fruits may contain a lot of added sugar. If you are buying dried fruits or berries, make sure there is no added sugar in them! Plums and raisins are naturally sweet enough that you can use them to satisfy any cravings for sugar. These food products actually do not require any refined sugar added to them.

- **Berries:** strawberries, cherries, blackberries, blueberries, blackcurrants, cranberries, etc.
- **Roots:** carrots, garlic and different kinds of onions, radishes, celery, turnips, ginger, horseradish, parsnips and so on.
- **Nuts and seeds** (that you can easily gather from nature without cultivation)**:** almonds, pine nuts, walnuts, hazelnuts, cashew nuts, coconuts, pecans, macadamia nuts, pistachios and other nuts; pumpkin seeds, sunflower seeds, and sesame seeds. These nuts and seeds are truly healthy, but just make sure that you don't eat packs and packs of them and avoid buying any salted or roasted nuts and seeds! Peanuts are not on this list because they are in fact legumes and not nuts.
- **Herbs and spices:** parsley, cilantro, dill, basil, grated pepper, cinnamon, bay leaves, coriander, cloves, rosemary, cumin, marjoram, oregano, peppermint, thyme, cardamom, mustard and a lot more. In place of refined salt, use sea salt!
- **Oils** (for salads and cooking)**:** avoid refined vegetable oils because there are a lot of far healthier alternatives available that go well with a Paleo diet such as olive, almond, coconut, avocado, sesame seed or walnut oils.
- **Eggs**

- **Drinks:** drinks suitable for this diet include water, freshly squeezed juices without added sugar, coconut milk, almond milk, coffee and tea (without sugar or sweeteners!) and smoothies.
- **Refined sugar substitutes:** raw honey, organic maple syrup, organic apple sauce, dried raisins and dates (without added preservatives), coconut sugar, ripe bananas, and agave nectar. In the recipes that follow, you will see how to use these products effectively.
- **Refined salt substitutes:** sea salt
- **Milk substitutes:** cashew milk, coconut milk, and almond milk.
- **Butter substitutes:** coconut oil (it has a solid consistency in room temperature and lower, but melts when heated, just like butter), mashed avocado (if not for greasing pots and pans), and almond butter.

So, to summarize the list of Paleo diet foods, always remember that if something can be gathered or hunted and if cavemen could eat it without using an agricultural means of growing, you can include it in your menu as well. Of course, we live in the21st century, and so this does mean that products, such as a glass of wine, won't hurt to drink, but **keep your use of these kinds of beverages in moderation.** These are further food products and beverages whose usage you should keep in check: wine, beer, tea, coffee, sweetening with honey or maple syrup; avoid eating too many nuts, dried fruits and berries and avoid using too much oil. Even if something is healthy, you should still keep a count of how often you are consuming these foods and beverages, Simply add them to your meals from time to time, but avoid making them the main ingredient in a dish by placing them at the center of your meal every day and you will be totally fine!

Let's get to it! - The Recipes

You now know plenty to get cooking, but before you do, here are some useful tips and advice before you dive in the collection of recipes that follows and start cooking:

- If you use canned foods that contain a lot of salt or sugar, soak and drain them before adding them to the Paleo slow cooker or dishes. Another option is to look for these products at farmers markets or read the labels on cans to find the best organic options.

- Browning meat and some vegetables like onions and carrots in a pan before putting it in a slow cooker will enhance the flavor, but you can prepare meals in a slow cooker without browning as well.

- It's pretty tempting to look into the pot from times to time as your meal cooks, but if the recipe doesn't ask you to check on it, try to keep the lid on to avoid letting out any heat.

- If you are unable to cover all the vegetables in the liquid before adding them to the slow cooker, it is useful to remember that vegetables shrink and release their natural juices so this will ensure that they cook well. If you add more water (or other liquids) than indicated in recipes the results of your dish may be that it is too watery.

- It's not a bad idea to add more of the suggested spices, including the sea salt, close to the end of cooking, because tastes tend to blend well in a slow cooker and you might not taste your favorite spices in there.

Remember: the calorie count provided with each recipe does not include optional ingredients and it will change if you replace one product with another!

Here you will find slow cooker recipes for all meals. Some of them will ask for you just to put different ingredients in the slow cooker and turn the heat on, while other recipes will have a slightly longer preparation time before cooking, but the latter will take no longer than 15-20 minutes of your time and the delicious results by cooking in your slow cooker makes those extra few minutes of preparation all worthwhile.

Breakfast Dishes

1. Overnight Sausage Pie

Servings: 4

Calories per serving: 429

Ingredients:

- 1lb organic pork sausage
- 8 eggs
- 1 medium-sized onion
- 3 cups fresh baby spinach
- 2 teaspoons dried basil
- 1 tablespoon garlic powder
- Pepper to taste
- Olive oil

Method:

1. Break the sausages, whisk the eggs and dice the onion.
2. Grease the slow cooker and add all of the ingredients to it. Stir to combine well, cover with a lid and leave to cook for 6-8 hours, until you wake up for a warm and tasty breakfast!

2. Sweet Apple Crunch

Servings: 8

Calories per serving: 374

Ingredients:

- 8 small apples
- 1 cup dates
- 1 cup dried cherries
- 1 cup pecan nuts
- Pinch of nutmeg
- Pinch of cinnamon
- Pinch of pumpkin pie spice
- ¼ cup coconut oil
- ¼ cup honey (or agave nectar)
- ½ cup water

Method:

1. Core the apples and cut them into four pieces. Chop the dates.
2. Put the apples, chopped dates, dried cherries and pecan nuts into the slow cooker. Sprinkle the spices over the fruit and nut mixture.
3. In a small pan, heat the honey along with the oil and pour over the fruit-nut mixture before adding half a cup of water to the slow cooker, covering it and allowing it to cook for about 6-9 hours on a low heat.

3. Sunday Morning Treat

Servings: 6

Calories per serving: 229

Ingredients:

- 6 apples
- ½ cup shredded coconut
- ½ cup coconut milk
- ½ cup raisins (dried without added sugar)
- 1 tablespoon vanilla extract
- 1 tablespoon cinnamon
- 1 teaspoon sea salt
- 1 tablespoon coconut oil
- Optional for serving: nuts of your choice

Method:

1. Remove the core from the apples and cut them into smaller pieces. In a bowl, combine all of the ingredients and stir to mix well.
2. Using the coconut oil, grease the slow cooker, transfer the apple mixture to the slow cooker, cover it with a lid and leave to cook overnight for 6-9 hours on a low heat.

4. Pork Sausage Casserole

Servings: 8

Calories per serving: 392

Ingredients:

- 1lb uncooked pork sausage meat of your choice
- 1 small-sized onion
- 1 cup coconut milk
- 12 eggs
- 1 small-sized butternut squash
- 1 tablespoon coconut oil (or other substance to grease pot)

Method:

1. Dice the onion, peel and dice the squash. In another bowl, mix together the coconut milk and beaten eggs.
2. Break down the sausage meat and brown it in a pan or skillet, add the diced onion and cook it together with the sausage meat until the onion gets tender.
3. Spread the coconut oil on the bottom and walls of slow cooker to grease it, then transfer all ingredients into the slow cooker, stir everything to blend well, put the lid on and leave it to cook on a low heat for 8-10 hours while you sleep.

5. Parsnip Casserole

Servings: 2

Calories per serving: 226

Ingredients:

- 2 cups grated parsnip
- 4 eggs
- Optional: sea salt and pepper to taste
- Optional for serving: pan-fried bacon strips

Method:

1. Clean and grate the parsnip.
2. In a bowl, beat and stir the eggs then add the parsnip.
3. Pour the egg-parsnip mixture into the slow cooker, cover with a lid and leave to cook overnight for about 8 hours on a low heat.
4. This breakfast dish is perfect when served with pan-fried bacon strips!

6. Overnight-Cooked Sausage-Egg Breakfast

Servings: 8

Calories per serving: 333

Ingredients:

- 12 eggs
- 1lb pork sausage (uncooked)
- 2 red bell peppers
- 1.5 cups spinach
- 2 green onions
- ¼ cup coconut milk
- ½ teaspoon sea salt
- ½ teaspoon pepper
- 1 tablespoon coconut oil

Method:

1. Dice the bell peppers, chop the spinach and thinly slice the green onions.
2. Put the sausages into a pan and brown them in coconut oil on a medium-high heat.
3. In a separate bowl, mix the eggs with the coconut milk, then add the sea salt, pepper, and spinach.
4. Grease the slow cooker with coconut oil, add the browned sausages to the bottom of the slow cooker, pour over the egg mixture and sprinkle the top with onions. Cover the cooker with a lid and leave for 7-8 hours on a low heat to enjoy for breakfast when you wake!

7. Chorizo Morning Burritos

Servings: 8

Calories per serving: 490

Ingredients:

- 1lb chorizo sausages
- 12 eggs
- ½ yellow onion
- 1 cup salsa sauce
- 1 teaspoon ground cumin
- 1 teaspoon garlic powder
- 1 teaspoon onion powder
- Sea salt and pepper to taste
- Paleo tortillas

Method:

1. Crumble the sausages and finely chop the onion.
2. Mix the beaten eggs with salsa sauce and spices in a mixing bowl.
3. Add all of the ingredients (except the tortillas) to the slow cooker and pour over the egg-salsa mixture. Cover the slow cooker and leave for 6-8 hours to cook on a low heat.
4. In the morning, serve the bake wrapped in the Paleo tortillas.

8. Breakfast Pork Meatloaf

Servings: 6

Calories per serving: 317

Ingredients:

- 2lbs ground pork
- 1 tablespoon coconut oil
- 2 onions
- 2 eggs
- ½ cup almond flour
- 2 tablespoons maple syrup
- 1 tablespoon garlic powder
- 2 teaspoons dried oregano
- 2 teaspoons ground sage
- 2 teaspoons dried thyme
- 2 teaspoons fennel seeds
- 2 teaspoons red pepper flakes
- 1 teaspoon paprika
- 1 teaspoon black pepper
- 1 teaspoon sea salt

Method:

1. In a bowl mix together all the seasonings and herbs.
2. Dice the onions and in a pan, heat the coconut oil and cook the onions for some minutes until they are translucent.
3. Add the cooked onions and beef into a bowl with the spices and herbs. Mix everything to blend well. Blending using your hands is the best option.

4. When mixed well, form a loaf from the meat mixture on a flat surface, and place it in the middle of the slow cooker, careful that it doesn't touch the sides of the pot. Cover the slow cooker and leave to cook for 3 hours on a low heat. If you are using a temperature probe, stop cooking when the internal temperature of the meatloaf has reached 150°F. Cook for longer if required.

5. Turn the heat off, remove the lid and leave in the slow cooker for a further 20-25 minutes before taking it out. Allow it cool, leave it in the refrigerator overnight and serve in the morning cut into slices. You can heat slices of the meatloaf in the morning using a greased pan or skillet and cooking the slices for approximately 1 minute on each side.

9. Pumpkin Pudding

Servings: 6

Calories per serving: 434

Ingredients:

- 3 tablespoons oil
- 3 cups pumpkin purée
- 2 cups coconut milk
- 3 eggs
- 2 teaspoons pumpkin pie spice
- ½ cup raw honey
- 3 tablespoons coconut flour
- 1 ½ tablespoons vanilla extract
- 1 teaspoon baking powder

Method:

1. Grease the bottom and lower walls of the slow cooker using coconut butter.
2. Combine all of the ingredients in the slow cooker and stir to blend well.
3. Put the lid on and cook for 7-8 hours on a low heat.
4. When the pumpkin pudding is ready, you'll notice that a crust has formed on top. Crush this and mix it into the pudding before serving.

10. Apple Butter

Servings: 10

Calories per serving: 188

Ingredients:

- 10-12 apples
- 1 cup organic apple juice
- 1 teaspoon lemon juice
- 1 teaspoon cinnamon
- ½ teaspoon vanilla extract
- ½ teaspoon nutmeg
- ¼ teaspoon ground cloves
- Pinch of sea salt

Method:

1. Peel, core and slice the apples, put them into the slow cooker and add the remaining ingredients. Stir, cover with a lid and leave to cook for 10 hours on a low heat.
2. After 8 hours have passed, blend the butter with hand blender to get a smooth consistency. Place the butter back into the slow cooker once again and leave to cook for a further 2 hours. You may wish to skip this step by simply leaving the apple butter to cook for 10-12 hours, but you will get a slightly different consistency.
3. Cool the apple butter before filling any jars. Once filled, the jars are ready to store. Apple butter makes a perfect breakfast along with a slice of one of our Paleo bread recipes.

11. Hearty Paleo "Sandwich"

Servings: 3

Calories per serving: 683

Ingredients:

- 1lb beef chuck roast
- 1 teaspoon onion powder
- 1 teaspoon garlic powder
- 1 teaspoon oregano
- 1 teaspoon ground rosemary
- ¼ teaspoon ground black pepper
- ¼ teaspoon sea salt
- Olive oil
- ½ cup water
- 1 tablespoon red wine vinegar
- 1 tablespoon Dijon mustard
- 6 large Portobello mushroom caps

Method:

1. Mix together all the herbs and spices and lightly rub the beef chuck roast with the herb-spice blend.
2. Heat the olive oil in a skillet, add the beef and cook each side for 4-5 minutes.
3. Transfer the beef roast into the slow cooker. Mix the water, vinegar and mustard and pour it into the slow cooker over the meat, cover with a lid and leave it to cook for 7-9 hours. Leave this recipe to cook overnight so as to get it nice and warm for breakfast. When it's ready, shred the meat.

4. Heat the oil in a pan and cook the Portobello mushroom caps for about 10 minutes.

5. Take one mushroom cup, put some shredded beef on top of before adding another mushroom cup. Your hearty breakfast sandwich is ready!

12. Slow Cooked Scotch Eggs

Servings: 3

Calories per serving: 423

Ingredients:

- 1lb ground pork
- 1 tablespoon spice mix (any kind of spices you wish. A mixture of cinnamon, nutmeg, ginger and allspice would fit well)
- ½ teaspoon sea salt
- ½ teaspoon ground black pepper
- 6 eggs, hard-boiled
- 2 tablespoons olive oil

Method:

1. Mix together the ground meat and all the spices.
2. Peel the hard-boiled eggs. Take a lump of ground meet, flatten it, put one whole egg on it and wrap the egg using the meat so as to form a ball with the egg inside. With 6 eggs you will get 6 Scotch egg-balls.
3. Heat the olive oil in a pan, add the egg-balls to it and brown them a bit. Grease the slow cooker with olive oil and transfer the egg-balls to the slow cooker. Leave them to cook covered for 2 hours on a high heat or 4-6 hours on a low heat. Refrigerate the egg-balls overnight and have them for breakfast.

13. Beef Bone Broth

Servings: 4

Calories per serving: 73

Ingredients:

- 2lbs beef bones
- 1 celery stalk
- 1 carrot
- 1 small onion
- 4 garlic cloves
- 2 bay leaves
- 2 tablespoons apple cider vinegar
- Pinch of salt
- Water

Method:

1. Chop the celery, carrot and onion, dice the garlic cloves and add them to the slow cooker. Place the beef bones over the vegetables, add the bay leaves, cider vinegar and a pinch of salt and pour the water into the slow cooker so as it just covers all of the ingredients. Then turn the heat on low and cook for 8-10 hours (or overnight) covered with a lid.
2. When it's ready, remove the bones, vegetables and bay leaves. You can use strainer to collect the broth. Your cup of light breakfast bullion is ready!
3. You can store the liquid in jars in the refrigerator and simply heat the broth to use on other mornings or use it in the preparation of soups and stews. Cold, the broth turns

to a jelly-like consistency leaving the grease on top in a solid consistency. Remove the grease and heat the remaining broth.

Snacks

14. Dark Chocolate Snack with Almonds

Servings: 10

Calories per serving: 246

Ingredients:

- 12 oz 72% cacao (or more) dark chocolate
- 1 cup almonds
- ⅓ cup coconut flakes

Method:

1. Prepare the slow cooker covering the bottom of it with parchment paper. Then place the almonds evenly at the bottom and scatter the coconut flakes over.
2. Break the chocolate into rough pieces and evenly lay this over the almonds and coconut flakes. Allow the chocolate to melt for 2 hours on a low heat keeping the lid on.
3. After 2 hours, turn off the heat and remove the lid. Leave it for about 3-4 hours to cool and harden. You can also take the chocolate out of the slow cooker together with the parchment paper and leave it in fridge to harden for a while. Cut into smaller portions before serving.

15. Sweet-Spicy Pecan Snack

Servings: 12

Calories per serving: 369

Ingredients:

- 16oz pecan nuts
- ½ cup coconut oil
- ⅓ cup raw honey
- 1-2 teaspoons ground cinnamon
- Pinch of dried, ground ginger
- Pinch of Sea salt

Method:

1. Melt the coconut oil in the slow cooker, then add the pecans and honey, and stir to coat the pecans. Cover the slow cooker and leave for 15 minutes to cook on a high heat.
2. After 15 minutes, remove the lid, stir once again, turn the heat to low and leave to cook uncovered for 2 hours.
3. After 2 hours, remove the pecans from the slow cooker, add the cinnamon, ginger and sea salt to the pecans, stir once again and leave to cool for 30 minutes–1 hour before eating.

16. Stuffed Mushroom Cups

Servings: 18

Calories per serving: 107

Ingredients:

- 18 mushroom cups (Portobello or Baby Bella fit well)
- 2 tablespoons olive oil
- ½ red onion
- 2 garlic cloves
- ½lb sausage patties
- Pinch of paprika
- ½ teaspoon ground black pepper
- 1 teaspoon sea salt
- 1 avocado
- ¼ cup fresh parsley
- Oil or butter of your choice (to grease the slow cooker)

Method:

1. Finely dice the onion, mince the garlic cloves, chop the parsley, peel and mash the avocado, and clean the mushrooms and remove their stems.
2. Heat the oil in a saucepan and add the removed mushroom stems, minced garlic and diced onion. Cook on a medium heat for 3 minutes. Then add the crumbled patties, paprika, pepper and sea salt, and lightly brown meat.
3. When cooked, remove from the heat and mix with the mashed avocado and parsley. With a little spoon, fill the mushroom cups with the mixture.
4. Grease the slow cooker with oil or a butter of your choice,

place filled mushroom cups in the slow cooker, cover with a lid and cook for 2-3 hours on a high heat or for 5-7 hours on a low heat.

17. Seed Snack

Servings: 4

Calories per serving: 174

Ingredients:

- ½ cup sunflower seeds
- ½ cup sesame seeds
- Pinch of chili powder
- Pinch of dried thyme
- Pinch of sea salt
- 1 tablespoon olive oil
- Water

Method:

1. Grind sunflower seeds to get a flour-consistency in a food processor, then add the sesame seeds, chili powder, thyme and sea salt. Mix these together well adding the olive oil and slowly pour the water in while stirring. You can pour in a little, stir and then pour some more. You're looking to get a dough-like consistency.

2. Prepare the slow cooker by lining it with parchment paper or another type of baking paper. Leave the sides longer, so that it will be easier to take the snack out together with the paper after cooking.

3. Using a spoon, evenly spread the dough on to the bottom of the paper as thin as possible, about $^{1}/_{8}$ inch thick would be perfect. Put the lid on and cook for about 1-2 hours on a high heat or for 4-5 hours on a low heat. Allow to cool before taking it out!

18. Sausage Bites

Servings: 4

Calories per serving: 220

Ingredients:

- 2lbs chicken sausage
- 2 small-sized onions
- 1 cup organic mango or apple-cranberry chutney
- ½ cup chili sauce

Method:

1. Cut the chicken sausage into 1-inch long pieces and slice the onions.
2. Place everything in the slow cooker, stir to coat the sausage pieces, then put the lid on and allow cook for2-3 hours on a high heat or for 5-6 hours on a low heat.

19. Italian Style Bite-Size Meat Balls

Servings: 20

Calories per serving: 290

Ingredients:

- 2lbs ground beef
- 1 ½ red bell pepper
- 6 garlic cloves
- 1 cup olives
- Onions with onion greens
- 4 tablespoons Italian seasoning
- 1 teaspoon sea salt
- 1 teaspoon ground black pepper
- 1 egg
- 1 tablespoon extra-virgin olive oil or coconut oil
- 24oz Paleo friendly pasta sauce
- 1 can diced tomatoes

Method:

1. Cut the whole red bell pepper into tiny slices and dice the remaining ½ of bell pepper. Mince the garlic, chop the olives and thinly slice the onions with onion greens.
2. Place the prepared vegetables (garlic, olives and onions), except the bell pepper slices, in one bowl. Add the Italian seasoning, sea salt and pepper. Mix these up using your hands to blend and form into bite-size balls.
3. In a skillet, heat the oil and add the meat balls. Brown them a bit on all sides, and transfer them to the slow cooker when browned.

4. Add the bell pepper slices and tomatoes to the slow cooker and then add the pasta sauce so that the meatballs are covered. Cover the cooker with a lid and leave to cook for 5-6 hours on a low heat.

5. Serve separately from the sauce.

20. Curried Almonds

Servings: 10

Calories per serving: 286

Ingredients:

- 1lb almonds
- 2 tablespoons coconut oil
- 1 tablespoon curry powder
- ½ teaspoon sea salt

Method:

1. Blanch the almonds: in a pot bring the water to a boil then add the almonds, leaving them to blanch for 1 minute. Remove the almonds, dry them and the skin peel off easily. Remove the skin from all the almonds.
2. Combine all of the ingredients in the slow cooker, stir well to coat the almonds, then cover the pot with a lid and cook for 3 hours on a low heat. Remove the lid and cook for 1 further hour uncovered on a high heat.

21. Almond-Date Bacon Wraps

Servings: 10

Calories per serving: 78

Ingredients:

- 10 raw almonds
- 10 pitted dates
- 10 bacon slices
- 2 tablespoons coconut oil

Method:

1. Stuff each date with 1 almond, and on a flat surface wrap the stuffed date in 1 slice of bacon. Repeat the method with the other dates, almonds and bacon slices. You can use a toothpick as pins to ensure that the almond-date bacon wraps won't open while cooking.
2. Melt the coconut oil and swirl it in the slow cooker to grease it. Add all the wraps to the slow cooker, cover it with a lid and cook on a high heat for 1-2 hours or on a low heat for 4-5 hours.

22. Chicken Fingers

Servings: 10

Calories per serving: 265

Ingredients:

- 10 skinless, boneless chicken tenders (finger-like slices)
- 1 egg
- 1 cup unsweetened coconut flakes
- ½ cup coconut or almond flour
- 1 teaspoon garlic powder
- ½ teaspoon sea salt
- ½ teaspoon curry powder
- Pinch of onion powder
- Pinch of cayenne pepper
- 1 tablespoon olive oil

Method:

1. In a shallow dish, break and beat the egg.
2. In another shallow dish, combine the coconut flakes and flour with the spices.
3. Cover the bottom and walls of the slow cooker with foil and grease the bottom with an oil of your choice.
4. Coat each chicken tender one by one with the coconut-flour mixture, then dip each one into the egg before placing them in the slow cooker. When all chicken-fingers are ready and they have been placed in the slow cooker, cover the slow cooker and cook on a low heat for 4-5 hours.

23. Shrimp Bites

Servings: 10

Calories per serving: 192

Ingredients:

- 1 lb peeled shrimp
- Zest of 1 lime
- ½ cup coconut flour
- 1 teaspoon sea salt
- ¾ teaspoon garlic powder
- ¾ teaspoon onion powder
- 2 eggs
- 1 cup macadamia nuts
- ¾ cup coconut flakes

Method:

1. Chop the macadamia nuts and grate the lime zest.
2. In a small bowl, mix together the lime zest, flour and spices. In another bowl, break and whisk the eggs. In a third bowl, combine the chopped macadamia nuts and coconut flakes.
3. Coat each shrimp using the ingredients in all three bowls: firstly in flour, secondly in egg, and thirdly in the macadamia-coconut mixture.
4. Place foil at the bottom of the slow cooker and add the coated shrimps to it. Cover with a lid and cook on a low heat for about 3 hours.

24. Simple Apple Snack

Servings: 4

Calories per serving: 56

Ingredients:

- 2 apples
- 2 tablespoons ground cinnamon

Method:

1. Core the apples and make apple rings by cutting them in no more than $^1/_8$ inch thick rounds.
2. Place the apples in the slow cooker, sprinkle with cinnamon, stir everything together, place the lid on the slow cooker, and leave to cook for 4 hours on a low heat.

25. Sausage Bites

Servings: 10

Calories per serving: 325

Ingredients:

- 3 ripe apricots
- 1 teaspoon lemon juice
- 2 teaspoons honey
- ½ cup Dijon mustard
- 2 lbs smoked sausage

Method:

1. Finely chop the apricots and mash them using a food processor or blender. Add the lemon juice, honey and mustard to the apricots, mixing them to blend well.
2. Cut the smoked sausage into bite-size pieces and add them to the slow cooker. Add the apricot mixture and stir to coat sausage. Cover the slow cooker and cook for about 3-4 hours, depending on the size of your slow cooker, on a low heat.

26. Maple Glazed Walnuts

Servings: 10

Calories per serving: 286

Ingredients:

- 3 cups raw walnuts
- 1 teaspoon sea salt
- ½ cup maple syrup
- 1 tablespoon coconut oil
- 1 teaspoon vanilla extract

Method:

1. Place the walnuts in the slow cooker, sprinkle the salt and drizzle the maple syrup, vanilla extract and coconut oil over them. Stir to blend, cover with a lid and cook on a low heat for 2-3 hours occasionally stirring. Cool before serving.

Soups and Stews

27. Creamy Parsnip Soup with Apples

Servings: 5

Calories per serving: 225

Ingredients:

- 2lbs parsnips
- 2 apples
- 1 medium-sized onion
- 2 garlic cloves
- 3 (14.5oz) cans of chicken broth
- ½ teaspoon sea salt

Method:

1. Peel the parsnips and cut, prepare the apples by peeling them, removing the core and cutting each apple into 4 pieces. Finely chop the onion and mince the garlic cloves.
2. Mix all of the ingredients in the slow cooker. Cover it with the lid and leave to cook for about 10-12 hours on a low heat. After this time, the parsnips should be tender.
3. Remove the soup from the heat and let it rest for about 10 minutes to cool. Then blend the soup in a blender to get a smooth consistency and serve the soup right after blending.

28. Beef-Turnip Stew

Servings: 5

Calories per serving: 222

Ingredients:

- 1lb raw (or frozen) beef
- 2 turnips
- 2 garlic cloves
- 1 medium-sized onion
- 3 celery stalks
- 2 carrots
- ½ can tomato paste (without added salt and added sugar)
- 4 fresh thyme springs
- 2 bay leaves
- 2 tablespoons of freshly chopped parsley
- 2 tablespoons apple cider vinegar
- Sea salt and pepper to taste
- Water

Method:

1. Cut the meat into cubes, dice the turnips, mince the garlic cloves, chop the onion, dice the celery stalks and cut the carrots into rounds.
2. Put all of the ingredients into the slow cooker and pour the water over it to fill about ¾ of the pot. Cover with the lid and leave to cook for 6 hours on a low heat.

29. Carrot Soup with Curry and Coconut Milk

Servings: 5

Calories per serving: 356

Ingredients:

- 2 tablespoons extra-virgin olive oil
- 1.5lbs carrots
- 1 leek
- 2 cups coconut milk
- 2 cups chicken broth
- 3 garlic cloves
- 1 teaspoon freshly grated ginger
- 1 teaspoon sea salt
- 1 teaspoon curry powder
- Pinch of cayenne
- For garnishing (optional): chopped onion greens or chives and red pepper flakes.

Method:

1. Peel and cut the carrots into rounds, slice the leek, mince the garlic cloves and grate the ginger.
2. Heat the oil in pan, add the carrots and leeks and cook them for about 10 minutes until they are a bit tender.
3. Add all the spices (garlic, ginger, sea salt, curry powder) into pan and stir everything together to mix well for about 3 minutes.
4. Transfer everything into the slow cooker adding the rest of ingredients and leave to simmer on a low heat for about 1 hour.

5. After the carrots are tender and 1 hour has passed, remove the soup from the heat, allow to cool, and using a blender, blend the soup, if desired. Serve the soup in separate bowls garnishing with chives and red pepper flakes!

30. Creamy Fire-Roasted Tomato Soup

Servings: 6

Calories per serving: 316

Ingredients:

- 4 tablespoons coconut oil
- 2 yellow onions
- 1 teaspoon ground coriander
- 1 teaspoon ground cumin
- 3 teaspoons curry powder
- ½ teaspoon red pepper flakes
- 1-2 teaspoons sea salt
- 2 (28oz) cans of fire roasted tomatoes
- 5 cups of water
- 1 can (14oz) coconut milk

Method:

1. Cut the onions into tiny slices, add them to a saucepan, and sauté the slices in melted coconut oil. When the onion tenderizes, add the coriander, cumin, curry powder, red pepper flakes and sea salt.
2. Then put the sautéed onions into the slow cooker, adding the tomatoes and the juice from the cans along with 5 cups of water. Put the lid on and leave to cook for 6 hours on a low heat.
3. After 6 hours, transfer everything to a blender and blend until smooth. Then put the purée back in the slow cooker, stir in the coconut milk and leave on a low heat for 1 more hour.

31. Mexican Chicken Soup

Servings: 6

Calories per serving: 169

Ingredients:

- 1lb chicken breast
- 1 red bell pepper
- 1 medium-sized onion
- 1 teaspoon oregano
- 2 teaspoons ground cumin
- 1 tablespoon chili powder
- 1 teaspoon sea salt (or to taste)
- 2 cups chicken broth
- 8 oz salsa verde (or other tomatillo sauce)
- 2 garlic cloves

Method:

1. Slice the bell pepper and remove the seeds, dice the onion and mince the garlic cloves.
2. Put the onions and bell peppers into the slow cooker ensuring that they are evenly laid out on the bottom and then put the chicken over the onions and bell peppers. Sprinkle the sea salt, oregano, cumin and chili powder over the chicken.
3. In a bowl, mix together the chicken broth, tomatillo sauce and minced garlic. Stir the mixture to blend well and then pour it into the slow cooker over the chicken breasts. Put the lid on and allow to cook for 6 hours on a low heat.
4. Shred the chicken and transfer it back to soup before serving!

32. Winter Soup

Servings: 6

Calories per serving: 357

Ingredients:

- 1.5lbs stew meat
- 1 butternut squash
- 4 carrots
- 5 garlic cloves
- 1 red onion
- 1 (14oz) can tomatoes (diced)
- 4 cups of water
- 2 tablespoons cumin
- 1 tablespoon dried oregano
- Ground black pepper to taste
- Sea salt to taste

Method:

1. Cut the meat into cubes, peel and dice the squash, chop the carrots into rounds, mince the garlic cloves and dice the onion.
2. Put everything into the slow cooker, stir it to combine, cover with the lid and leave to cook for 8 hours on a low heat.

33. Root-Ham Soup

Servings: 4

Calories per serving: 171

Ingredients:

- 2 oz spicy ham
- 2 small-sized carrots
- 1 parsnip
- 1 small-sized onion
- 1 garlic clove
- 2 tablespoons coconut oil
- 1 can (14oz) crushed tomatoes
- 3 cups water
- 1 bay leaf
- 1 fresh rosemary sprig
- Optional: sea salt and pepper to taste

Method:

1. Chop the ham in little cubes, dice the carrots, parsnip and onion, and mince the garlic clove.
2. On a medium heat, add the ham, parsnip, carrots onions and garlic with 1 tablespoon of coconut oil to a saucepan. Cook the ham it is crispy and the vegetables start to soften.
3. Grease the slow cooker with the remaining coconut oil (1 tablespoon), put in the crushed tomatoes and add the contents from the saucepan. Pour over the water, stir to blend, add the bay leaf and place a fresh rosemary spring on the top. Cover the slow cooker and leave on a low heat to cook for about 8 hours.

4. When ready, you can add sea salt and pepper just before serving.

34. Cabbage-Tomato Soup

Servings: 4

Calories per serving: 132

Ingredients:

- 1 small cabbage
- 2 medium-sized carrots
- 2 green bell peppers
- 5 celery stalks
- 2 garlic cloves
- 1 (8oz) can whole peeled tomatoes
- 1 can (24oz) organic tomato sauce
- 3 cups of water
- Optional: sea salt and pepper to taste

Method:

1. Prepare the vegetables: chop the cabbage, peel and cut the carrot into thick, and remove the seeds from the bell peppers and chop them; chop the celery stalks and mince the garlic cloves.
2. Add all of the prepared vegetables to the slow cooker, add the tomatoes with their juice, along with the tomato sauce and pour in the water. Stir everything together and leave to cook for 5 hours on a high heat or for 8 hours on a low heat.

35. Easy Chicken Soup

Servings: 6

Calories per serving: 304

Ingredients:

- 2.5lbs chicken pieces
- 2 large carrots
- 1 large-sized onion
- 3 celery stalks
- 2 bay leaves
- 2 fresh sprigs of parsley
- 1 teaspoon sea salt
- ½ teaspoon dried, crushed sage (you can replace it with basil or thyme if preferred)
- Pinch of black pepper to taste
- 4 cups of water
- Optional: 1 chicken bullion

Method:

1. Clean and cut the carrots into rounds, dice the onion, and cut the celery.
2. Add everything to the slow cooker, cover with a lid and leave to cook for 8-10 hours on a low heat.
3. When ready, take the chicken out of the soup, remove the meat from the bones, cut the meat into smaller pieces or shred before placing the chicken back into soup and serving.

36. Grilled Chicken Leftover Soup with Garlic

Servings: 7

Calories per serving: 238

Ingredients:

- 2-3 cups leftover meat from grilled chicken
- 1 whole garlic head
- 1 ½ onions
- 1 cup collard greens
- 3 broccoli stalks
- 8 cups chicken stock
- 1 cup organic tomato puree
- Sea salt, to taste
- Olive oil

Method:

1. Peel the garlic head and divide into cloves before mincing. Chop the onions, slice the broccoli, and finely chop the collard greens.
2. Heat the olive oil in a pan, add the onions and sauté them for 10 minutes. After 10 minutes, add the minced garlic, collard greens and broccoli and sauté, frequently stirring for a further 7 minutes. Then add the rest of the ingredients to the pan. When the mixture starts to boil, allow to simmer for 3 further minutes.
3. Transfer the contents of the pan to the slow cooker, turn the heat on low and leave to cook for about 5 hours.

37. Cold Beet Root Soup

Servings: 3

Calories per serving: 115

Ingredients:

- 3 medium-sized beets
- 3 carrots
- 2 garlic cloves
- ½ teaspoon sea salt
- ¼ teaspoon black pepper
- 3 cups water
- ½ teaspoon fresh dill
- 2 hard-boiled eggs

Method:

1. Peel and chop the beets and carrots. Add them to the slow cooker together with the minced garlic, salt and black pepper. Pour the water over the vegetables, cover the slow cooker and leave to cook on a high heat for 4 hours or on a low heat for 8 hours.
2. Grate the boiled egg whites and finely chop the dill. After the soup is ready and the beets are cooked through, remove it from the heat, add the eggs and dill and leave the soup to cool.

38. Sunny Pumpkin Soup

Servings: 6

Calories per serving: 135

Ingredients:

- 1 medium-sized pumpkin
- 2 parsnips
- 2 tablespoons coconut oil
- 1 large-sized onion
- 1 tablespoon minced ginger
- 1 garlic clove
- ½ teaspoon dried cilantro seeds
- ½ teaspoon ground cumin
- Sea salt and pepper to taste
- 3½ cups of water
- Optional for serving: freshly chopped chives and/or dried ham

Method:

1. Peel the pumpkin, remove the seeds and dice it into cubes. Clean and dice the parsnips, slice the onion, and mince the ginger and garlic clove.
2. In a saucepan on a medium heat, melt the coconut oil and add to it the onion, ginger, garlic, cilantro and cumin. Mix everything together and cook covered with a lid for 10 minutes, occasionally stirring. Then add the water to the saucepan and remove from the heat when it starts to boil.
3. Place the diced pumpkin and parsnip into the slow cooker, pour the hot mixture from the saucepan over them, add

sea salt and pepper (if desired) and leave the soup on a low heat for about 7-8 hours.

4. When the soup is ready, blend it in a blender or food processor to get a smooth consistency, and when serving, garnish each bowl with freshly chopped chives and dried ham pieces.

39. Green Chile Chicken Stew

Servings: 6

Calories per serving: 268

Ingredients:

- 1.5lbs boneless, skinless chicken
- 2 tablespoons olive oil
- 2 cups tomatillos
- 1 cup Green Chile sauce
- 2 cups chicken broth
- 2 roasted green chilies
- 1 medium-sized onion
- 4 garlic cloves
- ½ teaspoon cumin
- ½ teaspoon sea salt
- ¼ teaspoon black pepper
- 2 cups water

Method:

1. Dice the chicken into cubes. Remove the seeds from the roasted chilies and dice them. Peel the tomatillos and coarsely chop them, then dice the onion and garlic cloves.
2. Heat the olive oil in a pan over a high heat and add the chicken.
3. When the chicken is browned, transfer it to the slow cooker, adding the tomatillos and chili sauce too. Put the lid on and leave to cook for 2 hours on a low heat.
4. After 2 hours, add the rest of the ingredients to the slow cooker and leave to cook for 2 further hours covered with

a lid.

40. Mushroom-Mix Beef Stew

Servings: 6

Calories per serving: 422

Ingredients:

- 1 pack baby Portobello mushrooms
- 1 pack shiitake mushrooms (whole)
- 1 pack button mushrooms (sliced)
- 4 garlic cloves
- 1 cup pearl onions
- 1.5lbs stewing beef meat
- ⅓ cup balsamic vinegar
- 2 tablespoons red wine vinegar
- 2 tablespoons onion powder
- 1 teaspoon dried parsley
- 1 teaspoon dried sage
- 1 tablespoon dried rosemary
- Sea salt and pepper to taste
- 1 cup water
- 1 bay leaf

Method:

1. Peel and mash the garlic cloves and peel the pearl onions.
2. Place all the mushrooms, pearl onions and minced garlic to the bottom of the slow cooker, and then place the meat over the mushrooms.
3. In a bowl, combine the vinegars, seasonings and water. Stir to mix and then pour into the slow cooker over the mushrooms and meat. Add the bay leaf, cover the slow

cooker with a lid and leave on a low heat to cook for 7-8 hours.

41. Paleo Taco Soup

Servings: 4

Calories per serving: 306

Ingredients:

- Olive oil
- 1lb ground beef
- 1 red onion
- 4 garlic cloves
- 1 tablespoon chili powder
- 1 can (4oz) fire-roasted green chilies
- 4 tomatoes
- 1 cup salsa
- 2 cups chicken broth
- 1 teaspoon ground cumin
- ½ teaspoon paprika
- ¼ teaspoon dried oregano
- ¼ teaspoon red pepper flakes
- ¼ teaspoon onion powder
- ¼ teaspoon garlic powder
- Sea salt and pepper to taste
- Optional for serving: avocado slices

Method:

1. Peel and chop the onion, dice the tomatoes and mince the garlic cloves.
2. Brown the ground beef in a pan over a medium heat occasionally stirring it.
3. After the meat has been browned, add it to the slow

cooker. (You can drain the fat from the meat before transferring it, if desired). Add the rest of the ingredients to the slow cooker and stir to blend. Put the slow cooker on a low heat, cover it with a lid, and leave to cook for 6-8 hours.

4. Serve with avocado slices.

42. Broccoli Soup

Servings: 4

Calories per serving: 320

Ingredients:

- 5 cups broccoli florets
- 1 onion
- 4 celery stalks
- 2 garlic cloves
- 3 tablespoons coconut oil
- 2 tablespoons coconut flour
- 1 can coconut milk
- 1 cup chicken broth

Method:

1. Dice the onion, celery and garlic cloves. Cook them in a pan greased with coconut oil over a medium heat until they are tender. Transfer them to the slow cooker.
2. In the same pan, melt the coconut oil and add the coconut flour and milk. When the mixture has blended well, transfer it to the slow cooker.
3. Add the broccoli to the slow cooker, pour in the chicken broth, put the lid on and leave to cook for 7-8 hours on a low heat.

43. Sausage-Egg Soup

Servings: 8

Calories per serving: 377

Ingredients:

- 1lb pork sausage
- 1 onion
- 2 tablespoons olive oil
- 1 (14oz) can diced tomatoes
- 4 garlic cloves
- 1 teaspoon oregano
- 1 teaspoon thyme
- ¼ teaspoon chili flakes
- 3 cups water
- 1 cup coconut milk
- 8 hard-boiled eggs
- 1 bunch fresh kale
- Optional for serving: 1 bunch fresh chives

Method:

1. Ground the sausage and put it into the slow cooker.
2. Chop the onion and mince the garlic cloves. Heat one tablespoon of olive oil in a pan and sauté the garlic and onion. When they become translucent, add them to the slow cooker along with the remaining 1 tablespoon olive oil, tomatoes, oregano, thyme, chili flakes and water. Stir, cover with a lid and leave to cook for 5-6 hours on a low heat.
3. Some minutes before the soup is ready, slice the hard-

boiled eggs, coarsely chop the kale and finely chop the chives.

4. When the soup is cooked, add the coconut milk to the slow cooker and stir. Add in the kale and eggs, put the lid back on, and leave for a further 5 minutes. When the soup is ready, serve it with freshly chopped chives.

Meat Dishes

44. Cranberry-Apple Beef Roast

Servings: 6

Calories per serving: 122.7

Ingredients:

- 1lb round beef steak
- 5 cups unsweetened applesauce
- 5 cups cranberries
- 1 medium-sized onion
- 1 tablespoon ground cinnamon
- 1 teaspoon ground coriander seeds
- 1 tablespoon ground nutmeg
- Ground pepper to taste

Method:

1. Slice the onion and chop the cranberries.
2. Put all of the ingredients into the slow cooker, cover with a lid and leave to cook for 3 hours on a medium heat.

45. Hawaiian pork

Servings: 8

Calories per serving: 386.6

Ingredients:

- 2lbs pork shoulder
- ½ can cubed pineapple in water
- 1 tablespoon of fresh grated ginger

Method:

1. Put the pork shoulder into the slow cooker.
2. Add the canned pineapple to cover the top of the pork. Add the grated ginger and pour the water from the pineapple can over the ingredients in the slow cooker.
3. Allow to cook on a low heat for 7-8 hours and it's done!

46. Beef Roast with Cauliflower

Servings: 4

Calories per serving: 626.2

Ingredients:

- 2lb beef chuck
- 1 tablespoon extra-virgin olive oil or coconut oil
- 1 cup red wine
- 1 small carrot
- 2 celery ribs
- 1 small onion
- 1 small (about 400g) cauliflower head
- 2 garlic cloves
- About 10 fresh thyme sprigs
- 1 bay leaf
- Sea salt and pepper to taste

Method:

1. Turn on your slow cooker on a low heat and leave it to warm up.
2. Peel and cut the carrot, celery ribs, onion, and cauliflower into chunks and peel the garlic cloves.
3. Put the oil into pan and season the beef chunk with sea salt and pepper before placing the beef chunk in the pan. Brown it a little, then turn over and brown the other side as well. When it's done, place the beef chunk in the slow cooker right away.
4. Using the same pan where you browned the beef (you don't have to clean it, let the little bits stay there) pour

the wine in, and as soon as the first bubbles appear (this happens quickly), pour the wine over the beef in the slow cooker.

5. Add the rest of the ingredients – the carrots, celery, onion, garlic, thyme, bay leaf – to the slow cooker, except the cauliflower. Stir the ingredients into the liquid around the beef, put the lid on and leave to cook for 8 hours at a low heat.

6. After 8 hours, add the cauliflower florets to the slow cooker. Be sure to push them under the jus so that they are thoroughly covered. Replace the lid and cook for an additional 20 minutes at a low heat. Done!

47. Pork Tenderloin with Apples and Nutmeg

Servings: 4

Calories per serving: 356.7 (without optional ingredients)

Ingredients:

- 2lbs pork tenderloin
- 4 apples
- Crushed nutmeg
- Optional: raw honey (2 tablespoons)

Method:

1. Peel and slice the apples into about 1½ inch thick slices.
2. Cut the pork tenderloin into 3 pieces so that it can lay nicely in the slow cooker, then cut a little into the tenderloin so that you can stick a slice of apple into each cut. Make cuts about 1 inch distance from each other and place an apple slice into each slot.
3. Layer the apple slices on the bottom of the slow cooker, sprinkle the crushed nutmeg over them, put the prepared pork over the apples slices, sprinkle with more nutmeg, and add one more layer of apple slices over the pork, once again sprinkling everything with nutmeg. At this point, you can also add the honey, drizzling it over the other ingredients.
4. Cover with the lid and leave to cook for 8 hours on a low heat.

48. Savory Chicken with Cinnamon

Servings: 3

Calories per serving: 402.2

Ingredients:

- 2lbs chicken breasts or legs
- 2 bell peppers
- 1 onion
- 4 garlic cloves
- 2 teaspoons cinnamon
- 1 can chicken broth
- A pinch of nutmeg
- 2 teaspoons paprika

Method:

1. Slice the bell peppers, dice the onion, and mince the garlic cloves.
2. Put all of the ingredients into the slow cooker, stir well, cover with the lid, and leave to cook for 6 hours on a low heat or for 4 hours on a high heat.

49. Italian Style Shredded Beef

Servings: 5

Calories per serving: 538

Ingredients:

- 3 lbs beef roast
- 1 teaspoon of each of the following:

    - Garlic powder
    - Onion powder
    - Dried rosemary
    - Dried thyme
    - Oregano
    - Sea salt
    - Freshly ground pepper
- 1-2 tablespoons extra-virgin olive oil or coconut oil
- ½ cup water
- 1 tablespoon Dijon mustard

Method:

1. Mix all the herbs and seasoning (1 teaspoon of each) in a bowl and rub the beef roast with the mixture.
2. Heat the oil in a pan and add the meat. Brown the beef roast for about 5 minutes on each side.
3. Place the beef roast in a slow cooker, pour water over it, and cover with the lid. Leave to cook for about 9 hours on a low heat.
4. When it's cooked, remove the roast from the slow cooker and shred it, then add it to the cooking jus together with the mustard. Stir everything together and it's ready to be

served!

50. Tender Chicken Breasts with Rosemary

Servings: 4

Calories per serving: 164.4

Ingredients:

- 4 skinless, boneless chicken breast halves
- ½ cup dry white wine
- 1 tablespoon lemon juice
- 1 teaspoon balsamic vinegar
- 1 teaspoon granulated garlic (or garlic powder)
- Pinch of ground pepper
- Pinch of sea salt
- ½ cup fresh, diced tomato
- ½ teaspoon dried rosemary

Method:

1. In a small bowl, mix together the white wine, lemon juice, vinegar, pepper and sea salt. Stir it well to blend nicely.
2. Put the chicken breast halves into the slow cooker, pour the liquid mixture over them, cover the pot, and leave to cook for 6 hours over a low heat.
3. After 6 hours, add the tomatoes and rosemary, ensuring that you cover them in the cooking liquid and leave to cook for a further another 30 minutes.

51. Chicken breasts with Cabbage

Servings: 4

Calories per serving: 330

Ingredients:

- ½ a cabbage head
- 1 medium-sized onion
- 3 chicken breasts
- 2 cups fresh tomatoes

Method:

1. Shred the cabbage, slice the onions, dice the tomatoes and cut the chicken breasts into smaller pieces (each one in half is fine).
2. Put everything in the slow cooker, cover with a lid and leave to cook for 6 hours on a low heat.

52. Pepper Steak

Servings: 6

Calories per serving: 248.4

Ingredients:

- 2lbs lean steak
- 1½ red peppers
- 1 medium-sized onion
- 1 can mushrooms
- 1 can diced tomatoes
- ¼ cup salsa

Method:

1. Cut the meat into slices, slice the pepper, and chop the onion.
2. Place all of the ingredients together in the slow cooker, stir them to mix well and leave to cook for 7 hours on a low heat.

53. Moroccan Squash-Chicken

Servings: 5

Calories per serving: 210

Ingredients:

- 5 chicken thighs
- 4 teaspoons Moroccan spice blend
- 5 small-sized yellow summer squashes
- ½ cup dried apricots (no added sugar)
- 2 (14.5oz.) cans diced tomatoes (or tomatoes with garlic and onion are fine too)
- ½ cup golden raisins (without added sugar)
- 1½ cup chicken stock

Method:

1. To prepare the chicken, remove the skin and rub with each of the spice blends before placing it in the slow cooker.
2. Cut the squashes into rounds and the dried apricots into smaller pieces. Add the prepared squashes and apricots together with the rest of ingredients to slow cooker and stir everything. If there is any spice blend left from rubbing the chicken then add that too. Cover everything with a lid and on a low heat, leave the dish to cook for 6 hours or for 4.5 hours on a medium heat.

 84

54. Lamb Roast

Servings: 6

Calories per serving: 487

Ingredients:

- 2lbs lamb roast
- 16oz green chili
- 1 can (14.5oz) fire-roasted tomatoes
- 1 packet frozen bell peppers
- 1 tablespoon cumin
- 1 tablespoon paprika
- 1 teaspoon garlic powder
- 1 teaspoon chili powder
- Pepper and sea salt to taste

Method:

1. Defrost the bell peppers.
2. Place the lamb into the slow cooker. Dice the chili, tomatoes and bell peppers then add everything to the slow cooker covering the lamb. Stir everything to blend well, cover with the lid and leave to cook for 7 hours on a low heat.
3. Before serving the lamb, slice it.

55. Beef Ragu

Servings: 8

Calories per serving: 340

Ingredients:

- 1.5lbs beef rib meat without bones
- 1lb tomatoes (Roma tomatoes are a good choice)
- 8oz pack of baby carrots
- 10 garlic cloves
- Sea salt and pepper to taste
- ½cup red wine
- 3oz tomato paste
- Optional for serving: fresh basil leaves and pearl onions

Method:

1. Cut the carrots and tomatoes into small pieces and mince the garlic.
2. Cut the meat into chunks, sprinkle it with pepper and sea salt (if desired), and then place it in the slow cooker. Add the carrots and tomatoes to the sides of the slow cooker and sprinkle the garlic over the meat.
3. In another bowl, mix together the red wine and tomato paste and pour the mixture over the meat and vegetables in the slow cooker. Cover the slow cooker with a lid and cook for 7-8 hours on a low heat.
4. Stir once again before serving and garnish with pearl onions and fresh basil if you wish.

56. Sweet and Savory Honey Chicken

Servings: 6

Calories per serving: 347

Ingredients:

- 2lb boneless, skinless chicken breasts
- ⅔ cup chicken broth
- 1 onion
- 2 apples
- 2 teaspoons dry, ground ginger
- 1 teaspoon sea salt
- 1 teaspoon cinnamon
- ½ teaspoon ground black pepper
- ½ teaspoon paprika
- 2 garlic cloves
- 1 tablespoon raw honey
- 1 bay leaf

Method:

1. Slice the onion, remove the core from the apples and slice them. Crush the garlic cloves.
2. Pour the chicken broth into the slow cooker, add the onion slices and place the chicken breasts over the onion slices. Put the apples over the chicken, sprinkle everything with salt and the spices, pour the honey over, add bay the leaf and cover the cooker. Allow to cook for 9-10 hours on a low heat.

57. Easy Lemon-Pepper Chicken

Servings: 5

Calories per serving: 352

Ingredients:

- 2lbs boneless, skinless chicken breasts (or thighs)
- 2 teaspoons lemon pepper seasoning
- ½ teaspoons of sea salt (if desired)
- Pinch of ground black pepper
- 3 garlic cloves
- 3 tablespoons fresh lemon juice
- ¼ cup water

Method:

1. In a small bowl, mix together the lemon-pepper seasoning, sea salt and black pepper. Stir to blend well and rub each piece of chicken with this mixture. Place the seasoned chicken into the slow cooker.
2. Mince the garlic cloves and squeeze the lemon juice. Mix these together along with the water and pour into the slow cooker over the chicken.
3. Leave to cook for 5-6 hours on a low heat, covered with a lid.

58. Paleo Cabbage Rolls

Servings: 4

Calories per serving: 312

Ingredients:

- 12 cabbage leaves
- ½ onion
- 1 cup cauliflower
- 1lb ground beef
- 1 egg
- ¼ cup beef or chicken stock
- 1 tablespoon lemon juice
- 1 ½ cups tomato sauce (without added salt or sugar)
- Ground pepper to taste
- Sea salt to taste
- Water

Method:

1. Chop the onion, grate the cauliflower and squeeze the juice from the lemon (if not using ready-made juice).
2. Boil some salted water and add the cabbage leaves, cooking them for about 2 minutes to soften. Place the cabbage leaves under cold running water after removing them from the boiling water.
3. Combine the onion and cauliflower in a blender until you get rice-like consistency, then in a bowl, add this mixture to the ground beef, 1 egg, ¼ cup stock, pepper and salt. Mix it to blend well.
4. Divide the meat mixture into 12 equal pieces, then place

the bleached cabbage leaves one by one on a flat surface and fill each with the meat, fold leaf and roll to keep the meat inside. On completion, transfer all of the rolls to the slow cooker.

5. In another small bowl, mix together the lemon juice, tomato sauce and salt and pepper to taste (optional), pour the mixture into the slow cooker over the cabbage rolls, cover with a lid and leave to cook for 8 hours on a low heat.

59. Ginger-Pear Pork Chops

Servings: 5

Calories per serving: 370

Ingredients:

- 2 tablespoons coconut oil
- 4 pork chops
- ½ teaspoon cinnamon
- ½ teaspoon seasoning to your taste
- 1 tablespoon minced ginger
- 2 ripe pears
- 1 cup white wine (or water)
- 2 tablespoons apple cider vinegar
- 2 tablespoons honey
- Salt and pepper to taste.

Method:

1. Core the pears and cut them into chunks.
2. Melt one tablespoon of coconut oil in a pan and add the pork chops, sprinkling the seasoning over the meat. Brown the pork chops over a medium heat, about 2-3 minutes on each side, then transfer them to the slow cooker.
3. Using the same pan, add the ginger and pears, sauté them for 3-4 minutes, then add the wine, vinegar and honey. Stir to blend and leave to simmer on a medium-low heat for 5 further minutes, stirring occasionally.
4. Pour the liquid mixture over the pork chops in the slow cooker, cover with a lid and cook for 6 hours on a low

heat. If desired, add salt and pepper just before serving.

60. Classical Stuffed Bell Peppers

Servings: 4

Calories per serving: 391

Ingredients:

- 4 bell peppers
- 1lb ground meat
- ½ cauliflower head
- 1 onion
- 1 carrot
- 4 garlic cloves
- ¼ cup Italian seasoning
- Sea salt and pepper, to taste
- 6oz organic tomato paste
- ¼ cup water

Method:

1. Chop the cauliflower into florets, dice the onion and carrot and mince the garlic. Then put them into a blender or food processor and process until you get a rice-like consistency.
2. In a bowl, combine the vegetables with the ground meat, Italian seasoning, sea salt, pepper, and tomato paste. Be sure to blend them well.
3. Cut off the top parts of the bell peppers so that you have a pot with a lid, and remove the seeds from inside. Using a teaspoon, fill the peppers with the meat-vegetable mix and place all the filled peppers in a slow cooker.

4. Put the pepper lid tops onto the filled peppers, pour water into slow cooker to fill the bottom of the pot (do not pour the water directly onto the stuffed peppers), cover the slow cooker and leave to cook for 7-8 hours on alow heat.

61. Meatballs with Nuts and Mushrooms

Servings: 6

Calories per serving: 294

Ingredients:

- 1.5 lbs ground meat of your choice
- ½ onion
- 4 large-size mushrooms of your choice
- ½ cup of pecans or pine nuts
- 1 large-size carrot
- 3 garlic cloves
- 3 eggs
- ⅓ cup almond flour
- 1 teaspoon sea salt
- ½ teaspoon dried oregano
- ½ teaspoon seasoning of your choice (optional)
- 1lb fresh spinach
- 1 can (14oz) organic tomato sauce

Method:

1. Finely chop the mushrooms and onion, crush the nuts, peel and grate the carrot and mince the garlic cloves.
2. Prepare the slow cooker by pouring a little of the tomato sauce into it to cover the bottom. Cover the sauce by layering the spinach leaves over it.
3. In a large bowl, mix together all the remaining ingredients, leaving the remainder of spinach and tomato sauce for later on. It's easier to mix these ingredients by hand in order to blend well.
4. Form little meat balls from the mixture and place them

into the slow cooker in one layer. When the first layer is done, pour over some more tomato sauce and layer some more spinach over the meatballs before adding the next layer of meatballs over that. The number of spinach and meatballs layers depends on how big the slow cooker is that you're using.

5. When you have placed all the meatballs into the slow cooker, pour the remaining tomato sauce and spinach leaves over the meatballs, put the lid on, and leave to cook for 6 hours on a low heat.

62. Spicy Mexican Ribs

Servings: 4

Calories per serving: 452

Ingredients:

- 1.5lbs beef ribs
- 2 teaspoons garlic powder
- 2 teaspoons ground cumin
- 2 teaspoons paprika
- 1 teaspoon chili powder
- 1 teaspoon cinnamon
- 1 tablespoon adobo chilies
- 2 tomatoes
- 2 tablespoons organic tomato sauce
- 3 tablespoons raw honey
- 2 tablespoons olive oil

Method:

1. Chop the tomatoes and adobo chilies.
2. In a small bowl, blend all the spices together. Lightly rub the ribs with the spice blend and place the ribs into the slow cooker. Add the tomatoes and chilies.
3. Mix the tomato sauce, honey and olive oil and then add the mixture to the slow cooker spreading it evenly over the ribs. Put the lid on and leave to cook on a low heat for 5-7 hours.

63. Balsamic Chicken

Servings: 4

Calories per serving: 424

Ingredients:

- 8 skinless, boneless chicken thighs
- 1 tablespoon fresh basil
- 1 teaspoon onion powder
- ½ onion
- Sea salt and pepper to taste
- 4 garlic cloves
- ¼ cup balsamic vinegar
- Bunch of fresh rosemary
- ¼ cup coconut oil

Method:

1. Chop the basil and rosemary, mince the garlic cloves and slice the onion.
2. In a small mixing bowl, blend the basil, onion powder, sea salt and pepper. Lightly rub the chicken thighs with the mixture.
3. Add the coconut oil to the slow cooker and then add the onion slices and minced garlic as well as the prepared chicken thighs. Pour the balsamic vinegar over the thighs and finally sprinkle the chopped rosemary over the dish.
4. Put the lid on and leave for about 4-5 hours on a high heat or 6-8 hours on a low heat to cook.

64. Minty Lamb with Nuts

Servings: 6

Calories per serving: 346

Ingredients:

- Olive oil
- 2 onions
- 1 green pepper
- $^1/_8$ cup pine nuts
- 3 garlic cloves
- 2lbs ground lamb
- 1 teaspoon paprika
- 1 teaspoon cumin
- ¼ cup fresh mint
- Optional: Sea salt and pepper to taste.

Method:

1. Finely chop the onions and green pepper, mince the garlic cloves, and finely chop the mint.
2. Heat the olive oil in a saucepan and add the chopped onions, green pepper and pine nuts to sauté for about 5 minutes. Then add the garlic and allow to sauté for a further 3 minutes.
3. Add the meat, paprika and cumin to the pan, stirring the ingredients as you do so, and brown the meat for about 7-10 minutes occasionally stirring the mixture.
4. Transfer the contents of the pan into the slow cooker, cover with a lid, turn the heat on low and cook for 4 hours.

5. Finely chop the fresh mint, and after 4 hours, stir in mint. If you wish to also add sea salt and pepper, do so at this point, then your minty lamb with nuts is ready to serve. Great served with a green salad.

65. Moroccan Chicken

Servings: 8

Calories per serving: 606

Ingredients:

- 3 tablespoons coconut oil
- 4lbs chicken thighs
- 1 tablespoon freshly grated ginger
- 3 garlic cloves
- 2 yellow onions
- ⅓ cup freshly mashed apricots (or organic apricot purée)
- 1 lemon
- 1 can (14oz) tomato sauce
- 1 teaspoon ground ginger
- 1 teaspoon cumin
- ½ teaspoon paprika
- ⅓ cup almond butter
- 1 teaspoon sea salt
- 3 cinnamon sticks
- Water

Method:

1. Mash the ripe apricots if you are not using ready-made apricot purée. Grate the ginger, mince the garlic and slice the onions. Squeeze the juice from the lemon.
2. Heat the coconut oil in a pan and cook both sides of the chicken over a medium-high heat for 6-8 minutes. When it's done, transfer the chicken to the slow cooker.
3. In the same pan, add the grated ginger, garlic, and onions.

After cooking them for about 2 minutes add these to the slow cooker over the chicken.

4. Remove the pan from the heat and using the same pan still, add the apricot mash, lemon juice, tomato sauce, ground ginger, cumin, paprika, salt, and almond butter. Stir to blend well and deglaze the brown bits from the frying pan. Then pour this sauce into the slow cooker over chicken.

5. Pour water into the slow cooker to just cover the meat. Add the cinnamon sticks, place the lid on the slow cooker and turn on to a low heat. Leave to cook for 7-8 hours.

66. Paleo Lasagna

Servings: 8

Calories per serving: 423

Ingredients:

- 2 tablespoons olive oil
- 1 bell pepper
- 2 cups mushrooms of your choice
- 1 large-sized onion
- 1lb ground beef
- 1lb Italian sausage
- 1 can (28oz) crushed tomatoes
- 1 (28oz) can whole peeled tomatoes
- 2 garlic cloves
- 2 tablespoons dried oregano
- 1 tablespoon garlic pepper
- 1 tablespoon dried basil
- 1 butternut squash

Method:

1. Finely chop the onions and zucchinis. Slice the mushrooms, remove the seeds from the bell peppers and dice them, Cut the sausage into pieces and mince the garlic cloves.

2. Place a skillet over medium heat and heat the olive oil. Add the bell pepper, mushrooms and onion, allowing them to sauté while you partially cook the ground beef and sausage. When the vegetables in the skillet are tender and the meat is browned, transfer the meat into

vegetable skillet and add the tomatoes, garlic and herbs. Stir to blend and allow to simmer for a further 5-6 minutes.

3. Peel the squash and the remove seeds, then cut it in half-inch thick strips cutting it lengthwise to make lasagna "noodles".

4. Add a layer of meat-vegetable mixture to the slow cooker then layer the squash "noodles" over it. Add another layer of the meat-vegetables mix and cover it with layer of "noodles" until everything is layered in your slow cooker. When complete, put the lid on, and cook for 4-6 hours at a low heat. Take into account that you will need more hours for the dish to cook if you are using a small slow cooker with more lasagna layers, and less if your slow cooker is bigger and you have arranged the dish with less layers.

67. Almond-Olive Chicken Thighs

Servings: 4

Calories per serving: 265

Ingredients:

- 1 tablespoon olive oil
- 4 skinless, boneless chicken thighs
- 10 olives
- ½ cup raw almonds
- ½ onion
- 1 garlic clove
- ½ teaspoon chili powder
- ½ teaspoon cumin
- ¼ teaspoon black pepper
- ½ cup chicken broth

Method:

1. Coarsely chop the onion and mince the garlic clove.
2. Pour olive oil into the slow cooker to cover the bottom and add the chicken thighs.
3. In a bowl, mix the rest of the ingredients, stir them to blend, and then pour the mixture into the slow cooker. Stir the contents in the slow cooker to coat the chicken, put the lid on, turn the heat on low, and leave to cook for 8 hours.

Vegetable Dishes

68. Cauliflower-Garlic Mash

Servings: 3

Calories per serving: 29

Ingredients:

- 1 cauliflower head
- 3 cups water
- 4 garlic cloves
- 1 bay leaf
- Sea salt and pepper to taste

Method:

1. Divide the cauliflower into florets, peel the garlic cloves and put them into the slow cooker. Then add the water, bay leaf and about 1 teaspoon of salt. Cover the cooker with the lid and leave to cook on a low heat for 5-6 hours.
2. When it's done, remove the bay leaf and drain the liquid off. Use a blender or a potato masher to get a creamy purée, and add some pepper and salt to taste before serving.

69. Squash Mash

Servings: 6

Calories per serving: 63

Ingredients:

- 1 cup water
- 1 cup sun dried tomatoes
- 2 medium sized squashes
- 1 tablespoon tomato paste
- 2 teaspoons cumin
- 1 teaspoon garlic powder
- 1 teaspoon chili powder
- 1 teaspoon cayenne pepper
- Sea salt and pepper to taste

Method:

1. Place the dried tomatoes in 1 cup of water and leave them to soak for 1 hour or more.
2. Peel the squashes, remove the seeds and dice them, before putting them into the slow cooker. Add the soaked tomatoes with the water they were soaking in and stir in the cumin. Then cover the slow cooker with the lid and leave to cook for 3 hours on a low heat.
3. After 3 hours, when squashes are ready, add the rest of spices and blend everything using either a masher or simply a spoon.

70. Slow Cooked Root Vegetables

Servings: 6

Calories per serving: 215

Ingredients:

- 3 carrots
- 2 parsnips
- 2 red onions
- 2 garlic cloves
- 1 teaspoon oregano
- 1 teaspoon dried basil
- ½ cup coconut oil
- ½ cup water
- Optional: Sea salt and other spices

Method:

1. Peel and cut the carrots and parsnips, slice the onions, and mince the garlic cloves.
2. Combine everything in the slow cooker and stir to blend. Then cover the cooker with a lid and leave to cook on a low heat for 5-6 hours.

71. Sweet Acorn Squash

Servings: 5

Calories per serving: 235

Ingredients:

- 1 large acorn squash
- ½ cup raw honey
- 4 tablespoons coconut oil
- 1 teaspoon cinnamon
- 1 teaspoon ground nutmeg
- ½ cup water

Method:

1. Cut the squash into halves and remove the seeds.
2. In a small bowl mix together the honey, cinnamon and nutmeg. If you are using solid honey, heat it to melt.
3. Spread the honey-spices mixture over the top of each squash half. Add two tablespoons of solid coconut oil on each half, then place each squash half on foil and wrap each of them separately in the foil.
4. Place the wrapped squash halves into the slow cooker with the top upside, pour water onto the bottom of the slow cooker, cover with a lid and cook on a high heat for 4 hours or 6-9 hours on a low heat.
5. When it's tender and ready to serve, scrape the tender part and serve in the same "squash bowl".

72. Easy Slow Cooked Cabbage

Servings: 4

Calories per serving: 73

Ingredients:

- 1 cabbage head
- Water
- Sea salt to taste
- Optional: other seasonings to taste

Method:

1. Cut the cabbage into wedges and put into the slow cooker. And sea salt and seasoning if desired.
2. Pour the water into the slow cooker, enough to cover the cabbage. Cover with a lid and leave to cook for 8-10 hours.

73. Marjoram Mushrooms

Servings: 6

Calories per serving: 160

Ingredients:

- 1lb mushrooms
- ½ cup coconut butter
- 1 tablespoon marjoram
- 1 teaspoon chives
- ½ cup chicken broth
- ¼ cup dry white wine
- Sea salt and pepper to taste

Method:

1. Clean the mushrooms and if they are too big, slice them. Chop the chives.
2. In a bowl, mix together the marjoram, chives, broth, wine, salt and pepper. Stir to mix.
3. Place the mushrooms on the bottom of the slow cooker and sprinkle pieces of coconut butter over them. Pour the liquid mixture over the mushrooms, cover the slow cooker and leave to cook for 5-6 hours on a low heat.

74. Lemony Beetroot

Servings: 6

Calories per serving: 133

Ingredients:

- 2lbs beets
- 2 tablespoons honey
- 2 tablespoons olive oil
- 2 tablespoons fresh lemon juice
- 1 tablespoon cider vinegar
- ½ teaspoon ground black pepper
- ¾ teaspoon sea salt
- 2 sprigs fresh rosemary
- ½ teaspoon grated lemon rind

Method:

1. Peel the beets and cut them into wedges before placing the prepared beets in the slow cooker.
2. In a small mixing bowl, mix together the honey, olive oil, lemon juice, cider vinegar, pepper and salt. Mix them well and add these to the slow cooker, placing them over the beets.
3. Add the rosemary sprigs, cover and leave to cook for 8 hours on a low heat.
4. After 8 hours, when the beets are tender, remove the dish from the slow cooker, add the rosemary and lemon rind, and stir to mix.

75. Vitamin Packed Carrots

Servings: 8

Calories per serving: 163

Ingredients:

- 3lbs carrots
- ½ cup honey
- 2 tablespoons water
- ½ teaspoon sea salt
- 2 tablespoons coconut oil
- ½ teaspoon grated orange rind

Method:

1. Clean and prepare the carrots by cutting them diagonally in 2-3 inch pieces.
2. Transfer the carrots to the slow cooker, and then add the honey and water. Stir to coat the carrots. Add the and solid coconut oil pieces over carrots. Put the lid on and leave to cook for 8 hours on a low heat.
3. When the carrots are ready, add the grated orange rind, stir well and serve.

76. Slow Cooked Brussels sprouts

Servings: 3

Calories per serving: 160

Ingredients:

- ½lb Brussels sprouts
- 1 apple
- ½ red onion
- 1 tablespoon Balsamic vinegar
- 1 tablespoon Dijon mustard
- 1 tablespoon ground black pepper
- 1 teaspoon salt
- 2 tablespoon coconut oil
- ¼ cup water

Method:

1. Chop off the ends of each Brussels sprout and cut each into halves. Core and chop the apple and finely chop the onion. Put them all into the slow cooker.
2. Add the rest of the ingredients to the slow cooker, stir them to coat and blend well. Turn the heat on low, cover with a lid and leave to cook for 5 hours.

77. Curried Veggie Soup

Servings: 5

Calories per serving: 161

Ingredients:

- 1 medium-sized cauliflower head
- 3 bell peppers: yellow, orange and red
- 1 yellow onion
- Half-inch piece of ginger
- 2 teaspoons curry powder
- ½ teaspoon sea salt
- ¼ teaspoon cayenne pepper
- 1 cup coconut milk (unsweetened)
- 2 cups water (or broth)
- 2 cups fresh baby spinach leaves

Method:

1. Cut the cauliflower into florets or half-inch pieces, remove the seeds from the bell peppers and dice them, cut the onion in half and slice it, and then grate the ginger.
2. Combine the cauliflower, bell peppers, onion, ginger, curry powder, sea salt and cayenne pepper in the slow cooker, pour the coconut milk and water over them, and stir to mix. Cover the slow cooker with a lid and leave to cook for 6-7 hours on a low heat.
3. When it's ready, turn the heat off, stir in the spinach leaves, cover with a lid for 2-3 minutes, and then your curried veggie soup is ready to serve.

78. Roasted Vegetables

Servings: 5

Calories per serving: 94

Ingredients:

- 2 bell peppers
- 3 small-sized zucchini
- 2 whole garlic heads
- 2 tablespoons olive oil
- ½ teaspoon sea salt
- 1 teaspoon herbs/seasoning of your choice

Method:

1. Cut the bell peppers and zucchinis into large slices and peel the garlic cloves.
2. Add oil to the slow cooker, swirl it to spread the oil around, and then add the vegetables and seasoning. Stir everything to blend and coat. Cover with a lid and cook for 6 hours on a low heat or 3 hours on a high heat. You should check on the vegetables every hour and give them a stir.

79. Green Vegetable Side-Dish

Servings: 5

Calories per serving: 152

Ingredients:

- 4 tablespoons coconut oil
- 1 large-sized onion
- 1 medium-sized cucumber
- 2 medium-sized zucchinis
- 2 bell peppers: 1 green and 1 red
- ½ cup apple cider
- Sea salt and pepper to taste

Method:

1. Slice the onion, cut the cucumber in half, remove the seeds and slice it. Remove the seeds from the zucchini and slice it. Deseed the bell peppers and cut them into strips.
2. Melt the coconut oil in a pan, add the onions, and sauté over a medium heat until they are tender. Then add the cucumber, zucchini and bell peppers, stir in the apple cider and season with salt and pepper. Sauté for about five minutes (do not let them brown). Ensure that you stir the ingredients occasionally.
3. Transfer everything to the slow cooker, cover with a lid and leave to cook for 4-6 hours on a low heat.

80. Red Cabbage with Cranberries

Servings: 6

Calories per serving: 146

Ingredients:

- 1 medium-sized red cabbage
- 2 cups cranberries
- 2 medium apples
- 1 large-sized onion
- ½ cup organic apple juice
- 4 tablespoons red wine vinegar
- 2 tablespoons raw honey
- 1 teaspoon sea salt
- ½ teaspoon ground thyme
- ½ teaspoon cinnamon
- ¼ teaspoon ground black pepper

Method:

1. Coarsely chop the cabbage, mash the cranberries into a purée, peel the apples, remove the core and chop them coarsely, and cut the onion in to two and slice each half. Put all of these ingredients into the slow cooker.
2. In a bowl, mix together the apple juice, vinegar, honey and all the herbs and spices. Stir to blend well and then pour them into the slow cooker. Stir the contents in the slow cooker to coat well, put the lid on and cook for 6-8 hours on a low heat.

81. Squash-Apple Treat

Servings: 8

Calories per serving: 138

Ingredients:

- 3lbs butternut squash
- 4 apples
- ¾ cup dried cranberries
- ½ small-sized onion
- 1 tablespoon ground cinnamon
- 1 tablespoon ground nutmeg

Method:

1. Peel the squash, remove the seeds and cut it into cubes. Peel, core and chop the apples, finely chop the onion and add them all to the slow cooker.
2. Add the cranberries, cinnamon and nutmeg to the slow cooker and stir everything to combine. Cover the slow cooker and cook on a high heat for 4 hours or on a low heat for 8-9 hours. If happen to be at home, stir the mixture a couple of times while it's cooking.

82. Caramelized Squash Cubes

Servings: 4

Calories per serving: 113

Ingredients:

- 2 tablespoons coconut oil
- 1lb butternut squash
- 2 teaspoons red pepper flakes
- Pinch of ground black pepper
- Pinch of sea salt

Method:

1. Peel the squash, remove the seeds and dice into half-inch cubes
2. Melt the coconut oil and swirl it around the slow cooker to grease. Then add the squash-cubes, red pepper flakes, black pepper and sea salt. Cook uncovered for 1–1½ hours on a high heat or for 3-4 hours on a low heat, stirring it couple of times.

83. Simple and Fast Slow Cooker Asparagus

Servings: 4

Calories per serving: 56

Ingredients:

- 1lb asparagus spears
- 2 garlic cloves
- 1 tablespoon freshly squeezed lemon juice
- 1 tablespoon olive oil
- Sea salt and pepper to taste

Method:

1. Clean the asparagus and cut off approximately 1 inch from the bottom of each spear. Place them into the slow cooker.
2. Peel and mince the garlic cloves, and add them to the slow cooker over the asparagus.
3. Squeeze the lemon and add it to the slow cooker. Add the salt and pepper and drizzle olive oil over the ingredients in the slow cooker. Cover with a lid, turn the heat on low and cook for 2-3 hours if you are using larger asparagus spears, or for 1-2 hours if you're using younger and smaller asparagus spears.

84. Slow-Cooked Borscht

Servings: 6

Calories per serving: 208

Ingredients:

- 1 tablespoon olive oil
- 2 onions
- 2 carrots
- 4 celery stalks
- 2 garlic cloves
- ½ teaspoon salt,
- 1 (28oz) can chopped tomatoes (with juice)
- 3 medium-sized beetroots
- 1 tablespoon coconut sugar
- 3 cups water
- 1 small cabbage head
- 1 tablespoon vinegar of your choice (red wine vinegar is absolutely fine here too)

Method:

1. Finely chop the onions, dice the celery and carrots, mince the garlic cloves, peel and dice the beetroots, and finely shred the cabbage.
2. Heat the olive oil in a skillet, adding the onion, carrots and celery to it. Cook for 6-7 minutes on a medium heat until the vegetables tenderize. Then add the garlic and salt and cook for a further minute before transferring the cooked ingredients to the slow cooker.
3. Add the tomatoes, beetroot, sugar, and water to the slow

cooker. Stir everything to combine, put the lid on and leave to cook for 6 hours on a low heat.

4. After 6 hours, add the shredded cabbage and stir in the vinegar. Cover the pot again and cook for an additional 30 minutes.

85. Eggplant in Tomato Sauce

Servings: 6

Calories per serving: 80

Ingredients

- 2 large eggplants
- 1 onion
- 2 garlic cloves
- 1 can (28oz) diced tomatoes
- 6oz organic tomato paste
- ½ cup dry red wine
- 1 teaspoon dried oregano
- ¼ cup fresh basil

Method:

1. Peel the eggplants and cut them into half-inch pieces. Finely chop the onion and garlic cloves as well as the basil. Add these to the slow cooker.
2. Drain the tomatoes before adding them to the slow cooker and add the rest of the ingredients. Stir and then cover the slow cooker with a lid and leave to cook on a low heat for 6-7 hours.

86. Almost Bavarian Cabbage

Servings: 8

Calories per serving: 238

Ingredients:

- 1 large red cabbage head
- 2 medium-sized onions
- 6 medium-sized apples
- 2 teaspoons sea salt
- 2 cups hot water
- 6 tablespoons coconut oil
- 3 tablespoons honey
- ⅔ cup cider vinegar

Method:

1. Coarsely chop the cabbage and onions. Peel the apples and cut each into quarters. Place the cabbage, onions, and apples into the slow cooker and sprinkle with sea salt.
2. In a bowl, mix together the hot water, coconut oil, honey, and vinegar. Stir to melt and blend well, and then pour the liquid into the slow cooker. Cover with a lid and leave to cook for 8-10 hours on a low heat.

87. Stewed Tomatoes

Servings: 4

Calories per serving: 141

Ingredients:

- 7 ripe tomatoes
- 2 tablespoons coconut oil
- 1 medium-sized onion
- ¾ cup chopped celery
- 1 green pepper
- 2 tablespoons coconut sugar (or another Paleo-friendly sweetener)
- 1 bay leaf
- 1 teaspoon sea salt
- $^1/_8$ teaspoon pepper
- Optional for serving: finely chopped parsley

Method:

1. To peel the tomatoes, bring the water to a boil and place tomatoes in the pan for 20 seconds before transferring them to cold water. Remove the skin, slice them into 4 pieces and place them into the slow cooker.
2. Thinly slice the onion, chop the green pepper and celery, and add them to the slow cooker with the rest of the ingredients. Stir to blend. Cover the slow cooker with a lid and cook for 8 hours on a low heat.

88. Carrot Pudding

Servings: 6

Calories per serving: 168

Ingredients:

- 4 large carrots (cooked)
- 1 small onion
- 3 eggs
- 1 cup almond milk
- 1 tablespoon honey
- ½ teaspoon salt
- ¼ teaspoon nutmeg
- 1 tablespoon coconut oil

Method:

1. Grate the cooked carrots and finely chop or grate the onion. In a separate bowl, beat the eggs.

2. Grease the slow cooker with coconut oil and add the carrots and onion to it.

3. Add the milk, honey, salt and nutmeg to the beaten eggs. Stir them to blend and then pour the mixture into the slow cooker. Stir everything again, put the lid on and cook on a high heat for 3-4 hours or on a low heat for 6-9 hours.

Breads and Desserts

89. Stuffed Cinnamon-Apples

Servings: 4

Calories per serving: 416

Ingredients:

- 4 green apples
- ½ cup coconut butter
- ¼ cup almond butter
- 2 tablespoons cinnamon
- Pinch of nutmeg
- Pinch of sea salt
- 4 tablespoons unsweetened, grated coconut
- ½ cup dried apricots or dates
- 1 cup water

Method:

1. Core the apples, grate the coconut and cut the dried apricots (or dates) into small pieces.
2. Mix the melted coconut and almond butter with the salt, cinnamon and nutmeg, and add the dried fruits. Stir well and using a teaspoon, fill the cored apples with this mixture.
3. Put the apples in the slow cooker. Add the water (do not pour the water over the stuffed apples), then add the shredded coconut, sprinkling it on the top of each apple as well as some more cinnamon if desired. Leave the apples

to cook for about 2½ hours on a low heat.

90. Pears in Coffee- Sauce

Servings: 8

Calories per serving: 125

Ingredients:

- 6 pears
- ¼ cup maple syrup
- 2 tablespoons cocoa powder (unsweetened)
- ⅔ cup coconut milk (unsweetened)
- ⅓ cup strong coffee
- 2 tablespoons coffee liqueur (or replace it by adding 2 tablespoons of strong coffee)

Method:

1. Cut the pears into 4 pieces, remove the peel and cores and place the prepared pieces in the slow cooker.
2. In another bowl, mix the rest of the ingredients, stirring them to combine well, and then add the mixture to the slow cooker, pouring it over the pears. Put the lid on and cook for 3-4 hours on a low heat.
3. Serve the pears along with the delicious coffee-coconut cooking sauce poured over them.

91. Zucchini Bread

Servings: 10

Calories per serving: 189

Ingredients:

- 3 eggs
- 1 cup organic applesauce
- 1 cup honey
- 1 teaspoon baking soda
- ½ teaspoon baking powder
- 3 cups almond flour
- ¼ teaspoon sea salt
- 3 teaspoons vanilla extract
- 2 teaspoons cinnamon
- 1 large zucchini (2 cups grated zucchini)
- Optional: 1 cup grated dark chocolate
- Cooking spray (that doesn't contain soy. Alternatively, replace it with coconut butter or another Paleo-friendly greasing ingredient to grease the slow cooker)

Method:

1. Peel and grate the zucchini, grate the dark chocolate (if you choose to use it) and melt the honey if you do not have runny honey.
2. Take a bowl to make the batter: add the beaten eggs, applesauce and honey, and stir to blend. Then mix the batter with the rest of the ingredients.
3. Grease the slow cooker with cooking spray and transfer the zucchini dough to the slow cooker. Cover it with the

lid and leave to cook for 2-3 hours on a low heat.

92. Almond Flour Brownie Bites

Servings: 10

Calories per serving: 284

Ingredients:

- ⅓ cup water
- 2 cups dried dates
- 2 cups almond flour
- ¾ cups cocoa powder (unsweetened)
- ½ cup coconut milk
- 2 eggs
- 2 teaspoons baking soda
- 2 teaspoons baking powder
- 1 teaspoon sea salt
- 2 teaspoons vanilla extract
- ½ cup coconut oil

Method:

1. Process dates in a food processor to get a smooth consistency.
2. Combine all the ingredients, except the coconut oil, in a bowl and stir to blend well.
3. Use the coconut oil to grease the slow cooker, and pour the prepared mixture into the cooker evenly, spreading it with a spoon. Cover the slow cooker and cook for 5-6 hours on a low heat.
4. When it's ready, remove brownie dough from the heat and allow to cool for about 30 minutes to cool. Using a spoon, take out the dough from the slow cooker bit by bit and form into small bite-size balls.

93. Pumpkin Bread

Servings: 10

Calories per serving: 182

Ingredients:

- ¼ cup coconut flour
- 1 cup almond flour
- ½ teaspoon sea salt
- ½ teaspoon baking powder
- ½ teaspoon cinnamon
- 3 tablespoons pumpkin pie spice
- 4 eggs
- ½ cup coconut oil
- ½ cup mashed pumpkin
- 2 tablespoons raw honey (or another Paleo-friendly sweetener)
- $^1/_8$ cup pumpkin seeds
- Paleo-friendly cooking spray or another Paleo-friendly oil/butter to grease the slow cooker

Method:

1. In a mixing bowl, combine the coconut flour, almond flour, sea salt, baking powder, cinnamon and pumpkin pie spice. Stir to blend.
2. In another bowl, beat the eggs and add melted coconut oil, blend them and then add the pumpkin purée and sweetener of your choice. Once blended, slowly stir the mixture, adding in the flour-spice blend and mix well.
3. Grease the bottom and lower walls of the slow cooker, transfer the batter into the slow cooker and top it with

pumpkin seeds. Cover the slow cooker and leave to cook on a low heat to cook for about 6 to 8 hours. Use a toothpick to check that the pumpkin bread is cooked through.

4. Before removing the pumpkin bread from the slow cooker and slicing it, allow the bread to cool for a while.

94. Coconut Bread

Servings: 10

Calories per serving: 180

Ingredients:

- ¾ cup coconut flour
- 6 eggs
- ½ teaspoon sea salt
- ½ cup coconut oil
- Optional: 2 tablespoons raw honey

Method:

1. Melt the coconut oil and mix it with the eggs and salt. Slowly add the coconut flour and melted honey (if you are using it). Stir to blend well.
2. Turn the slow cooker on to a low heat, pour the coconut-egg batter into the slow cooker, cover it and leave to cook for 7 to 9 hours.

95. Honey-Zucchini Pie

Servings: 10

Calories per serving: 231

Ingredients:

- 1 cup shredded zucchini
- 8 eggs
- ½ cup coconut oil
- 5 tablespoons raw honey
- 2 teaspoons vanilla extract
- 3 teaspoons cinnamon
- 1 teaspoon ground ginger
- ½ teaspoon salt
- ¾ cup coconut flour
- 1 teaspoon baking powder
- Paleo friendly cooking spray or any other Paleo- friendly alternative to grease the slow cooker

Method:

1. In a bowl, combine the zucchini, eggs, honey, vanilla extract, cinnamon, ginger and salt. Melt the coconut oil and stir it into the mixture. When everything is well blended, pour in the coconut flour and baking powder.
2. Grease the slow cooker and evenly pour in and spread the batter. Cover and cook on a low heat for 4-6 hours. Use a toothpick to check that the pie is cooked through.

96. Blueberry Morsels

Servings: 5

Calories per serving: 231

Ingredients:

- 3 cups shredded coconut (unsweetened)
- 16oz frozen blueberries (unsweetened)
- 2 egg whites
- 1 teaspoon vanilla extract
- 2 drops almond extract

Method:

1. Over a medium heat, defrost the frozen blueberries in a saucepan. Stir them frequently until they start to boil, allowing the liquid to reduce and the berries to thicken in consistency.
2. In a bowl, mix together the shredded coconut, blueberries, and vanilla and almond extracts. Separate the egg-whites, add them to the mixture, and blend.
3. Grease the slow cooker. If preferred, you can also place cooking paper on the bottom of the slow cooker. Using a teaspoon, form little balls and place them on the bottom of the slow cooker. Cover with a lid and cook for 1-1.5 hours on a high heat or for about 4 hours on a low heat.

97. Healthy Paleo Apple Sauce

Servings: 16

Calories per serving: 59

Ingredients:

- 10 medium-sized apples
- ½ cup water
- ¼ teaspoon cinnamon
- Optional: ½ cup honey

Method:

1. Peel the apples, remove the core and chop them.
2. Put the apples into the slow cooker and add the water. Put the lid on and leave to cook for 6 hours on a low heat.
3. If you are adding the honey as well, add this after 6 hours of cooking, stir and leave to cook for a further 30 minutes.
4. When ready, sprinkle the sauce with cinnamon. This sauce goes perfectly with any of the Paleo breads.

98. Sweet Walnut-Cranberry Bread

Servings: 10

Calories per serving: 149

Ingredients:

- ½ cup coconut flour
- 1 teaspoon baking soda
- ¼ teaspoon sea salt
- 5 eggs
- ½ cup agave nectar (or another Paleo-friendly sweetener)
- 1 tablespoon vanilla extract
- ½ cup grapeseed (or coconut) oil
- ½ cup walnuts
- 1 cup frozen cranberries

Method:

1. In one bowl, mix together the baking soda and coconut flour.
2. In separate bowl, mix the eggs with the sweetener, vanilla extract and oil. Then mix together the ingredients from both bowls adding the chopped walnuts and cranberries as well.
3. Grease the slow cooker with grapeseed or coconut oil, pour in the batter, cover with a lid, and leave to cook on a low heat for about 10 hours. Cooking time depends on the size of your slow cooker and how thick the layer of batter is, so check the bread with the toothpick to ensure that the bread has cooked through to the middle.
4. Allow to cool before slicing and serving.

99. Berry Crumbles

Servings: 4

Calories per serving: 205

Ingredients:

- 3-4 cups frozen or fresh berries
- 3 tablespoons coconut oil
- 1 cup almond flour
- 1 tablespoon honey

Method:

1. In a small saucepan, melt the coconut oil and add the honey and almond flour. Remove from the heat and stir until the ingredients crumble.
2. Put the berries into the slow cooker and sprinkle the honey crumbles over them. Cover the slow cooker with a lid, turn the heat on to low, and leave to cook for 2 hours. Cool for a while before serving.

100. Cinnamon Apples with Nuts

Servings: 6

Calories per serving: 335

Ingredients:

- 2 tablespoons coconut oil
- ½ cup pecan nuts
- ⅔ cup walnuts
- ¼ teaspoon nutmeg
- ¼ cup almond flour
- 1½ tablespoons cinnamon
- 6 apples
- ½ cup raisins (without added sugar)
- 1 tablespoon vanilla extract

Method:

1. Core the apples and chop them. Chop the pecans and walnuts.
2. In a small saucepan, melt 1 tablespoon of coconut oil, add the nuts, nutmeg, and almond flour, as well as 1 teaspoon of cinnamon. Stir to blend.
3. Grease the bottom of the slow cooker using 1 tablespoon of coconut oil. Add the chopped apples, raisins, vanilla and 1 tablespoon of cinnamon. Stir to mix well and then drizzle over the previously prepared nut mixture.
4. Cover the slow cooker with a lid and leave it to cook for 4 hours on a low heat, or better still, on a high heat for 2 hours. After the suggested cooking time, remove the lid and allow to cook for a further thirty minutes uncovered.

The cinnamon apples with nuts are now ready to serve!

101. Not-So-Slow Banana dessert

Servings: 6

Calories per serving: 413

Ingredients:

- 8 bananas
- 1 cup coconut flakes
- ½ cup walnuts
- ½ cup coconut oil
- 1 teaspoon vanilla extract
- ¼ cup lemon juice
- 2 teaspoons lemon zest
- Optional for serving: coconut cream

Method:

1. Cut each banana into 3-4 pieces. Coarsely chop the walnuts.
2. Add the pieces of bananas to the slow cooker and sprinkle the walnuts and coconut flakes over them.
3. In a saucepan, melt the coconut oil and stir in the vanilla extract, lemon juice and lemon zest. Pour this mixture into the slow cooker over the bananas.
4. Cover the slow cooker with a lid and allow the bananas to cook for 1-2 hours on a low heat until they are tender. Take into account that the cooking time will be less if you are using really ripe bananas, as they will become too tender and won't keep their solid form. Tastes great served topped with coconut cream!

Conclusion

Many people are lactose and gluten intolerant, so the dairy and grain free Paleo diet is a great and healthy solution that ensures that you receive all the necessary nutrients to keep your energy levels up while staying healthy and fit.

The Paleo diet and slow cooking goes hand in hand in this busy world where time more often than not means money. If in your case time is money, slow cooking brings them both to you because you are not required to spend hours in the kitchen even when preparing large amounts of food. It is no wonder that electric slow cookers are so popular nowadays – they save you time and cook your meals even while you are sleeping or out of home for work, without you spending too much on electricity.

"Paleo Slow Cooker Recipes: Easy, Delicious, Gluten-free Hands-Off Cooking For Busy People" is a world of flavors and healthy foods without putting too much of an effort into cooking. It's a myth that Paleo means eating meat for all your meals and not catering for that sweet tooth. It's a myth that slow cookers are only for meat and stews – there is a lot more you can prepare in a slow cooker starting from healthy breakfasts that will cook while you sleep to breads and desserts to trigger your entire family's taste buds. Breakfasts, snacks and appetizers, soups, stews, hearty meat and light vegetable dishes, delicious desserts and breads are all to be enjoyed – the options for Paleo slow cooking are pretty impressive, and in particular, these recipes keep you doing what you'd prefer to be doing rather than cooking.

Made in the USA
Lexington, KY
03 December 2015